I0820182

"Here in Birmingham, Alabama, I often teach about the civil rights movement as the most effective faith-based movement for social change in American history. Justin Giboney honors such heroes as Fred Shuttlesworth and commends their example for today in this informative, provocative book."

Collin Hansen, editor in chief and vice president for content at The Gospel Coalition and host of the *Gospelbound* podcast

"Justin Giboney has given us a masterpiece—a Christian, historical, political masterpiece. Giboney shows that the African American fight for justice was not just a church movement but a biblically based, unabashedly Christ-centered movement. Then, with the steadfast faith of God's Black disciples of the past serving as both standard and example, he addresses—and undresses—America's contemporary culture war. In reading this, we modern day Christians will be humbled but also inspired, inspired to follow their lead in bringing God's truth to bear on today's most vexing challenges."

Chris Broussard, sports reporter and founder of The K.I.N.G. Movement

"Justin Giboney is in a category all by himself—so is this book. Giboney is one of those emerging leaders who merits careful attention not merely because of charisma but more so from depth of insight and careful reflection. He's a strange mix of Tim Keller and Martin Luther King Jr. wrapped up in his own personality and voice. The church was born in the public square from the day of Pentecost onward. Sadly today, the church has come to view the public square as a boxing ring instead of a living room where we can have public discourse without having to vilify those we disagree with. This book charts a new path to engagement and witness for followers of Jesus in a public way. Giboney will make everyone uncomfortable at some point, but he will also make everyone think if they are willing."

Bob Roberts, president of the Center for Global Faith and host of the *Bold Love Podcast*

"In this bold and necessary work, Justin Giboney challenges the Black church to reclaim its historic role as a moral compass and cultural bridge. With theological depth and cultural clarity, he reminds us that our public witness is not about choosing sides in a culture war but about standing firmly on the side of truth, justice, and redemptive love. This book is a call to courage, conviction, and collective responsibility. It's not just a must-read. It is truly a revival of the spirit in print."

Barbara Williams-Skinner, president of Skinner Leadership Institute

"*Don't Let Nobody Turn You Around* is a fascinating look at the Black church's role in navigating cultural conflicts. The author proposes that believers are obligated to share the complete gospel without conforming to worldly ways. Historically, Christian leaders have faced the choice of engaging in divisive cultural battles or exemplifying kingdom values through their words and actions. This tension persists today, challenging believers to maintain a distinct and transformative public witness. The book emphasizes that Christians should not assign their witness to political or ideological groups, especially when such groups misrepresent Christian values. Instead, believers are called to pursue justice and speak truth in love, following the Black church's tradition of social action. I believe it is a must-read for believers who have influence in today's culture."

John K. Jenkins Sr., senior pastor of First Baptist Church of Glenarden

"This book calls us to draw wisdom from the past as we navigate the challenges ahead. It is a vital read—both timely and transformative!"

Lisa Victoria Fields, CEO of the Jude 3 Project and author of *When Faith Disappoints*

"Through brilliant historical analysis, personal storytelling, and practical wisdom, Giboney invites Christians to better steward our public witness. This book is encouragement for Christians on the front lines of political engagement, inspiration for those on the sidelines who've been hesitant of Christians being politically involved, and hope for those disillusioned by injustice. Drawing on a legacy of activism and pointing readers to the power of our faith, Giboney reminds you that your public witness matters and that God has always used his people to be change makers in the earth."

Sarita T. Lyons, author of *Church Girl: A Gospel Vision to Encourage and Challenge Black Christian Women*

"In our era of extreme polarization and political partisanship, Justin Giboney's close study of how the historic Black church held together orthodoxy, piety, and social justice is vital and instructive. Giboney moves us past superficial engagements with the high-profile leaders of the movement and acquaints us with lesser known but equally important pastors and activists like Fred Shuttlesworth and Fannie Lou Hamer. This book is required reading for every Christian who wonders how to be courageous and faithful amid the challenges we face in our present moment."

Tish Harrison Warren, Anglican priest and author of *Liturgy of the Ordinary* and *Prayer in the Night*

DON'T LET NOBODY TURN YOU AROUND

HOW THE BLACK CHURCH'S PUBLIC WITNESS LEADS US OUT OF THE CULTURE WAR

JUSTIN E. GIBONEY

FOREWORD BY ESAU McCAULLEY

An imprint of InterVarsity Press
Downers Grove, Illinois

InterVarsity Press
P.O. Box 1400 | Downers Grove, IL 60515-1426
ivpress.com | email@ivpress.com

InterVarsity Press® is the publishing division of InterVarsity Christian Fellowship/USA®. For more information, visit intervarsity.org.

Cover design: Faceout Studio, Jeff Miller
Interior design: Jeanna Wiggins
Cover image: © EZEEproject / DigitalVision Vectors via Getty Images

ISBN 978-1-5140-0842-3 (print) | ISBN 978-1-5140-0843-0 (digital)

Printed in the United States of America ♾

Library of Congress Cataloging-in-Publication Data
A catalog record for this book is available from the Library of Congress.

30 29 28 27 26 25 | 13 12 11 10 9 8 7 6 5 4 3 2 1

THIS BOOK IS DEDICATED TO

my late grandfather and grandmother,

Bishop Thomas L. Cooper and Willie Faye Cooper.

The Coopers attribute the long tenure of their marriage to a firm belief in the laws of God. "Our belief in God brought us together and it has kept us together. The Lord watches over and protects all that is good."[1]

CONTENTS

FOREWORD

ESAU McCAULLEY

BLACK CHRISTIANS AND MANY OTHER believers in the United States often face a conundrum. They look at the political options before them on the left and the right and wonder if these are the only two options. Do not misunderstand: the two parties that dominate American politics are not equally wrong about all things. They are just profoundly mistaken about particular things, each broken in its own unique way.

We look around and wonder, *Does any else notice this dilemma? Am I alone in seeing the problem?* Or, more pointedly, we ask ourselves: Am I crazy? Should I just pick up my rhetorical sword and do battle for my tribe like everyone else? This issue extends beyond politics, reaching into the heart of Christian theology and praxis. Are holiness, right living, and a high view of Scripture at odds with the pursuit of justice? Do I need to choose between personal piety—that is, love for Jesus—and public witness?

We feel lost, wondering what Christians are supposed to do in this moment when everything seems compromised and far from the way of Jesus. Are we supposed to detach ourselves from politics altogether? Should we chart some middle path between what we deem to be two extremes? Shall we become mushy moderates, as if the kingdom of God is found in the center?

Justin Giboney turns to the history of the Black Church to help us answer these and many other questions. *Don't Let Nobody Turn*

You Around helps us look back in order to move forward. Justin reminds us that we are not the first Christians to be asked to choose between false and damaging alternatives. The central stream of Black faith in the United States has long married orthodoxy (right belief about God) with orthopraxy (right action as seen in love of neighbor and concern for the disinherited).

This book is both prophetic—willing to speak plainly about the problems that we face—and charitable—he does not engage in polemics for the sake of polemics. It is bursting with historical knowledge, astute political insight, and deeply Christian reasoning. The sentences leap off the page, and the quality of the prose matches the adeptness of his argument.

In this book, Justin does not suggest that Christians in a pluralistic society shrink back from their core convictions or surrender them at the table of social respectability. He instead articulates a vision of principled engagement where we make common cause, even with people with whom we disagree. His goal, then, is not some middle ground, but walking in the way of Christ while acknowledging that because America is not the kingdom of God, it will always fall short of what it could be. It is for this reason that America will also always need the witness of the church, calling it to be better than it currently is. The Black Church did that in the past, the whole church can do that in this season of the life of the republic.

Justin's conviction is that the Black social witness should not remain trapped in the past or limited to one culture. The witness of the Black Church, set free from those who would mar her testimony to suit their needs, is a gift from the Black Church to the world. The wider community of believers must learn from that testimony, because God has invited the whole church to be witnesses to Christ and his kingdom. That is our call, and Justin is correct. We can let nobody turn us around.

INTRODUCTION

YOU'VE GOTTA MOVE

RECONSTRUCTION AND THE EMERGENCE OF THE BLACK CHURCH SOCIAL ACTION TRADITION

Tell the government,
when the Lord gets ready, you've got to move.

Brother Joe May

RICHARD H. CAIN, an African Methodist Episcopal pastor, was driven into civic engagement by a shepherd's concern for the flourishing of his congregation. He had no special passion for elected office, nor was he particularly fond of either political party. But even after slavery was abolished, South Carolina's unjust Black Codes were crushing his people's political and economic prospects. Furthermore, unreformed Confederates constantly threatened Black lives with impunity. For instance, during the Hamburg Massacre, White rebels targeted leaders in the Black community for lynching, then terrified Black children by offering to feed them the flesh of a recently murdered Black body.[1] It was clear that despite the Emancipation Proclamation, a darkness remained upon the nation. America needed a light, and Cain's parishioners at Emmanuel Church and Black Americans, in general, needed an advocate.

Few were as charismatic and well-respected as Cain, and the Fourteenth and Fifteenth Amendments had opened the door for

Black men to seek elected office.[2] As a talented writer and orator, he was well-suited to voice the aspirations and needs of his people in the public square, and given his unique gifts and the dire circumstances, refusing to engage might've seemed negligent. Accordingly, Pastor Cain would establish and become the editor of the *Missionary Record* newspaper, a faith-based publication focused on topics like suffrage, labor, education, and general reform.[3] He'd also join South Carolina's constitutional committee, where he was a part of a Black delegation advocating for freedom of speech and assembly, free public education for all races and classes, and the confiscation of Confederate rebel property for former slaves.[4]

Cain would eventually become one of the United States congressmen who'd help advance the Civil Rights Act of 1875, the country's first public accommodations law.[5] To accomplish this victory, he and other proponents defeated archrival Congressman Alexander Stephens, the former Vice President of the Confederacy and the future governor of Georgia. Known as "the brains of the Confederacy,"[6] he was intent on obstructing any legislation intended to move Black people closer to full citizenship.

During the congressional debate, Cain addressed Congressman William K. Robbins, a former Confederate Army major, who claimed White Southerners philanthropically tried to educate enslaved Blacks, but the "barbarians," as he put it, were incapable of improvement. Pastor Cain called out this lie and detailed how the South had actually done tried to create barbarians:

> What schoolhouse in all the South was open to the colored race? Point to one. Name the academy where you educated black men and black women as lawyers or doctors, or in any other department of science or art. . . . Name the teacher. I will name one. Her name was Missa Douglas. And for the attempt to educate those of our race she was incarcerated in

> prison, and remained there for five years. . . . Examine the laws of the South, and you will find that it was a penal offense for anyone to educate the colored people there.[7]

Robbins also said, the "negro race is the world's stage actor—the comic . . . that he laughs and he dances." Cain would address that comment as well and without returning insult for insult.

His speech would end on an aspirational and prophetic note, testifying to why he believed God placed the races in America together:

> I believe Almighty God has placed both races on this broad theater of activity, where thoughts and opinions are freely expressed . . . and develop every art and science that can advance the prosperity of the nation . . . to develop this great idea that all men are the children of one Father. We are here to work out the grand experiment.[8]

Cain believed in the US Constitution inasmuch as it affirmed the dignity that God bestowed on every human being, and any white supremacist who denied that was not only civically misguided, but morally wrong on that account. He not only made a compelling constitutional and moral case for equality under the law, his studied, meticulous performance debunked every premise underlying the idea of Black inferiority. Cain served as a living illustration. After all, how could he formulate such a cogent argument and win the debate if he were intellectually inferior?

As Cain pierced through logical fallacies, it seemed God was using his every word and turn of phrase to expose white supremacy as an affront to his design and eschatological plan. It had to take great courage and discipline for Cain to look the perpetrators of his people's genocide in the eye and tell the whole truth without sinning under the weight of his anger.

Second Corinthians 5:20 says, we are ambassadors of Christ "as though God were making his appeal through us." God speaking through our political and cultural engagement is serious business. This means that engagement belongs to God and is to be used for his purposes. It's part of our public witness, which is a precious and powerful gift. Our public witness is our testimony to the world about what is true and good and what is false and immoral. It tells others what we value, represent, and who we serve. It can teach, encourage, make peace, and tear down wicked institutions. It's more valuable than free expression alone, which is subject to vain beginnings and empty endings.

An anointed witness never returns void because it testifies to the source of all meaning and a design beyond human devices. A faithful witness summons our creativity to serve the Creator and partake in his divine masterpiece. You can hear it in the abolitionist's petition against the slave trader or the righteous prosecutor's indictment of the sex trafficker. Our testimony about God's will in the public square and the path to redemption and flourishing gives us purpose in an otherwise trifling existence.

However, our public witness can be squandered by selfish ambition or manipulated through indoctrination. It's susceptible to self-sabotage and can destroy us like Judas in the field of blood. If not stewarded prayerfully, it will be corrupted. It can be used for moral and intellectual improvement or weaponized for destructive purposes. We can waste our voice crooning about the empty freedom of pleasure seeking or wail a word that frees the captives—"We shall overcome someday!" It's never perfect but always redeemable. Even after three denials, St. Peter's witness became more forceful than his sword. Whether it's a signature on a petition, exposition from a pulpit, policy prescription in a legislative assembly, lessons from a lectern, investigative journalism in a periodical, economics in a business symposium, prose in a novel, or even satirical truth from a comedic stage, we can awaken and inspire the world by communicating our convictions publicly.

But our public witness is more than just verbalizing our convictions. It's also the application of those convictions in our actions. It's not just what we say, it's our attitudes and what we consistently do. It's what we value as demonstrated through the sacrifices we make. For example, in Exodus, when the midwives undermined the king's edict to murder all the Hebrew boys, their public witness proved they valued the lives of those made in the image of God more than they feared human authority (Exodus 1:1-21). Their faith wasn't just talk; it was evident in how they engaged society. Our witness tells people who we really are and what we sincerely represent. The harmony or disharmony between our convictions and our conduct informs them about the earnestness of our public witness. For example, when the church advocates for the Christian sexual ethic then covers up sexual abuse, we lose credibility because of the disconnect between our words and actions.

Richard Cain wasn't the only Black Christian driven to seek elected office. At the height of Reconstruction, around 2,000 African Americans held elected office, many of them Christian preachers like Hiram Revels, Henry McNeal Turner, Tunis Campbell, and George Freeman Bragg or Christian laymen like Robert Smalls. These were Black leaders whose oratory and political prowess were outstanding if not miraculous given the circumstances. Observers noted that the "African-influenced cadence of speech" was clearly influenced "by the preaching in black churches."[9]

They would master parliamentary procedure—becoming virtuosos in statecraft. Robert Smalls had been property under the law until he escaped slavery in 1862, and now he and other Black men were fashioning the law.[10] He was a former field hand who now had a policy pen in his palm.[11] The New York Times noted that they were often the best debaters in the legislature—blessed with common sense and rhetorical flourish.[12] One journalist said the

"African love of melody was noticeable in the harmony of [their] delivery."[13] In other words, their rhetorical techniques were soulful.

It's as if they'd taken the sacred desk and a Hammond organ, placed it in parliament, and made it their own. One might say they were accompanied by the Holy Spirit in the civic assembly. This is because the Black ecclesial tradition has always had a habit of bringing the church with them into the public square. Not in violation of the separation between church and state, but as a testament of the Lord's sovereignty in the sanctuary and in what would otherwise be secular jurisdiction.[14]

With moral imagination, these men helped create the framework of the Black Church social action tradition, which engaged the public square without separating their religion from sociopolitical advocacy—the church was the advocate. They met contempt with dignity and aspiration in a refusal to lower the moral standard in the civic context. They also modeled a commitment to facing a dangerous society with tenacity and grace based on a devout faith in the promises and commands of God. They took the ideals of the Founding Fathers, enlarging their scope to really include "all men," demonstrating a deeper commitment to "life, liberty and the pursuit of happiness."

Jesus was anointed "to proclaim good news to the poor . . . to set the oppressed free" (Luke 4:18). In the same spirit, Richard H. Cain and other Reconstruction-era Christian civic leaders were led to become advocates in the public square. The spiritual guided their social and political commitments. They were representatives of their church and their constituencies. Decades later, singer Brother John Sellers from Mississippi explained that pastors often appeared to be the only people able or willing to advocate for Black people in society. For instance, in areas where there weren't any Black lawyers, it was often the Black preacher "who would go to court and plead for you."[15] Their pastoral vocation called them to lead inside the church, and since the church was the predominant Black institution, their social standing in the community compelled them to lead outside the church.

We pursue the Great Commission through our public witness—"Therefore, go and make disciples of all nations" (Matthew 28:19). To share the whole council of God isn't an option, it's a command. To avoid conforming our thoughts, words, and actions to the world is also a command (Romans 12:2). If we're silent when it's time to bear witness to the truth or if our message loses its distinctiveness and becomes camouflaged in the world, then we're no good to the kingdom of God (Matthew 5:13). Christians should never assign our witness to others by allowing them to speak falsely on our behalf or by simply repeating faulty narratives. When we outsource our witness to a political party or ideological tribe and let them use our identities and platforms for ungodly purposes, we're wasting an inheritance and defying God's commands to do justice and speak the truth in love (Micah 6:8; Ephesians 4:15).

Christians, especially Christian leaders, have a crucial decision to make concerning our public witness. Will we clumsily choose sides in the toxic culture war that's destroying the American discourse? Or, in the spirit of the Black Church's social action tradition, will we have the dexterity to chart a different course that's distinctly Christian, choosing just and moral positions that defy the "conservative vs. progressive" framework rather than one of the two deficient sides?

There's a cross in the public square that belongs to neither the Left nor the Right. It's both weighty and light. Christians must carry it self-sacrificially with our witness in culture and politics. For our public witness is cross-bearing, which makes it both an obligation and a privilege. We are servants empowered by faith and led by moral imagination.

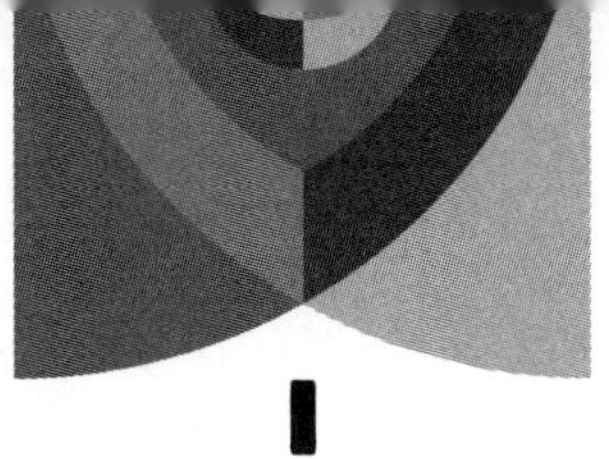

1

IT'S TIME TO MAKE A CHANGE

THE CIVIL RIGHTS GENERATION AND THE SPIRIT OF THE TRADITION

For our foreparents who died for us,
it's time to make a change.
Lord, working in the field from dawn till dusk,
it's time to make a change.

BOLD Mass Choir

MY MATERNAL GRANDMOTHER, Willie Faye, was born in Forest, Mississippi, in 1932. That's the same year segregationist Martin "Sure Mike" Conner was inaugurated as governor of Mississippi.[1] From Reconstruction to the 1950s, Mississippi had more lynchings than any other state in the Union. Accordingly, Willie Faye's parents kept a shotgun by the door to protect the family in case the Ku Klux Klan decided to pay them a visit and tried not to leave the house after sundown. Fearing the false allegations of looking at a White woman inappropriately, her first cousins, Billie and Buford, fled the state as teenagers. Yet, Conner, a Yale-educated lawyer, practically ignored the issue while endlessly railing against the federal government and President Roosevelt's New Deal for "meddling in the race question" and treading on states' rights.[2]

Named after her father, Willie Frazier, Willie Faye, or Faye for short, was the sixth of eight children. By natural disposition, she became the glue binding a house full of conflicting personalities together. She found herself playing the role of mediator, defusing in-house rivalries and settling disputes. The siblings would have to pick cotton to help make ends meet and they often went shoeless as they labored in the heat of the Mississippi Delta for depressed wages that weren't magically corrected by the invisible hand of the market. Early on, she vowed that her future children would never pick cotton or go shoeless.

Unlike Governor Conner, Faye would not attend an Ivy League school or any college at all. She'd leave high school at the age of sixteen to get married. According to her mother, this was the best option given the social location of a Black woman of her day and by this time, her family had uprooted and moved to Decatur, Illinois, in search of greater social justice and economic opportunities. She was one of millions of Black Americans who relocated from the South to the North in what's been called the Great Migration from 1910 through 1970.[3] According to Jonathan Frank, the editor of the National Baptist Union Review, a Black Baptist publication, the migration might've had social and religious implications. He compared it to the Hebrews being delivered from Egypt: "The migration of colored people to the North is a great religious movement. God's hand in it is almost visible."[4]

Interestingly, neither Faye nor any of her siblings liked talking about life in Mississippi. They wouldn't volunteer much information, and when one of her eldest nieces tried to document a family history, she was surprised how few memories they were willing to share about life before moving north. She had to pry, and her questions were sometimes met with vagueness or explicit rejection. It's as if looking back was almost forbidden. "Flee for your lives! Don't look back, and don't stop" (Genesis 19:17).

Before leaving school, Faye sang in the Colored Girls' Choir at Stephen Decatur High School. She also sang in the choir of her Black Pentecostal church and developed a passion for the formation and Christian education of children. Faye loved gospel music. Every Saturday morning when she cleaned the house, there was one voice her three children were sure to hear: Mahalia Jackson. Known as the Queen of Gospel Music, Jackson was her favorite artist—a muse Willie Faye would cherish in mundane, celebratory, and disheartening moments for decades. Her voice would pierce through denominational walls and inspire singers like Aretha Franklin. Dr. Martin Luther King Jr. would say, "A voice like [Mahalia's] comes along once in a millennium."[5] It's been described as not a voice, but a force of nature.

Mahalia, "Halie" for short, was born in New Orleans in 1911. She grew up in the Black Pearl section of the city in a three-room house with thirteen family members, including aunts and cousins. Her mother, Charity, died when she was five years old, leaving her with her Aunt Duke, a stern disciplinarian.[6]

Three of Mahalia's nicknames from childhood provide insight into her early social experience: "Hook" referred to her severely bowed legs and crossed feet, "Black" referred to her dark complexion, and "Warpee" was the name of a Native American character who walked around barefoot, as Mahalia often did because she couldn't afford shoes. While the nicknames were often repeated affectionately, they exposed real pain points in her life. Born with deformities, dark skin in a colorist society, and in poverty, Mahalia was about as far from privilege as one could get.[7] Her ascribed status didn't provide her with any advantages, but her faith, diligence, and her voice would distinguish her in due time.

Mahalia left school before finishing fourth grade to work and tend to family.[8] However, her experience overcoming her disadvantages in a harsh urban environment developed a "mother wit" that'd eventually make her a wise counselor and formidable businesswoman.[9] Throughout a very rough childhood, Mahalia always had the church. Her maternal grandfather, Paul Clark, was a Baptist preacher, and from a young age, she was known as a prayer warrior who almost never missed a church service. She sang her first hymn at four and was capturing the audience at Mount Moriah Baptist Church by fourteen.[10]

She would move to Chicago with her Aunt Hannah a year later on the Illinois Central Railroad. Chicago had been described to her as a majestic place of prosperity and culture—the promised land—by family members who'd moved or visited earlier.[11] When she first arrived, she was stunned when a White cab driver picked her up at her aunt's request. She wasn't used to being served by White people; she was only familiar with serving them. She planned to reenter school and train to be a nurse, but her work was limited to that of a domestic—cleaning houses.[12]

Mahalia was a dutiful congregant. Her friend, Brother John Sellers, said she would do almost anything for her pastor.[13] Willie Faye had a similar conviction, but perhaps with an additional motive. She was married to the man who pastored her church for most of her adult life, Rev. Thomas Lee Cooper from Brownsville, Tennessee. She'd stand faithfully beside this civil rights–era preacher for almost forty years until her death. He pastored in the Church of the Living God, the Pillar of Ground and of the Truth, also known as PGT Nation, a Black Pentecostal denomination.

Willie Faye and Mahalia shared a common American experience viewed through the lens of faith. Both Black women were born deep in the Jim Crow South and reared in the traditional Black Church. The stench of slavery still lingered in the air of their environment and was visible in the scars of the family members who shaped their worldview. Both were nurtured by elders who were formerly enslaved themselves.[14] They were cautioned by the wisdom of the enslaved and emboldened by the courage of those who'd survived America's original sin.

These women lived in an era that some have called America's Second Slavery.[15] Even after Emancipation, Black labor was still being stolen through the sharecropping system, and racial injustice was upheld in courts of partiality. Additionally, white supremacist defenders of the Lost Cause believed it their calling to literally terrorize the Black community to maintain political and economic dominance.[16] During the late nineteenth and early twentieth century, almost two or three Blacks were lynched every week in America.[17] As Willie Faye and Mahalia were coming into womanhood, the "progressive" eugenics movement was giving "false scientific legitimacy" to forced sterilization. As a result, tens of thousands of Black women were victimized by non-consensual sterilization, including civil rights leader Fannie Lou Hamer, who called it a "Mississippi Appendectomy."[18] They both journeyed to escape Jim Crow's jurisdiction, but would still endure racism with a different accent and Midwestern flavor.[19]

Willie Faye and Mahalia's story is the story of the Black Church's civil rights generation, a generation whose Christian faith and social action prowess provided us with perhaps the greatest illustration of moral imagination in America's history. For the purposes of this book, Willie Fay and Mahalia's generation are those who served as the base of the civil rights movement—the progeny of the enslaved and the fruit of the Black Church.

They were Black Americans for whom the Christian church served as the center of spiritual, social, and political life. This generation intersects substantially with the Silent Generation (1928–1945). However, those in the older segment of this cohort, like Rosa Parks and Mahalia Jackson, were born in the 1910s. This generation was born from roughly 1910 to 1940 with members like John Lewis being on the younger end. The Black Church is broadly defined as Christian denominations and congregations in America that are primarily led and attended by African Americans. While the Black Church was never a theological monolith, this book will refer to what Dr. Esau McCaulley describes as the mainstream of the Black ecclesial tradition, which was "unapologetically Black and orthodox."[20]

Socially and politically, their American experience was beset by the evils of Jim Crow—social exclusion, systemic denigration, lynching, and so on. They also suffered through the scarcity of the Great Depression, maneuvered through the Great Migration, and weathered the uncertainties of World War II. Willie Fay and Mahalia's generation was far from a product of peace and privilege. At the beginning of their lives, they were unequal under the law and even after a number of judicial and legislative victories, they still found themselves unequal in fact.

In a speech promoting the Civil Rights Act of 1965, President Lyndon Baines Johnson described some of the traits and the impact of Willie Faye and Mahalia's generation:

> The real hero of this struggle is the American negro. His actions and protests, his courage to risk safety and even risk his life have awakened the conscience of this nation. He has called upon us to make good the promise of America. And who among us can say that we would've made the same progress were it not for his persistent bravery and his faith in American Democracy.[21]

The following are some primary characteristics, among others, that distinguished them and their tradition of social action from the rest of the American cultural and political landscape.

1. They connected the spiritual with sociopolitical advocacy.[22]
2. They upheld social justice and moral order—which means they didn't fit into the conservative-versus-progressive culture war binary.

3. They acknowledged the potential for wickedness in themselves, not just in others.
4. They were led by moral imagination and refused to treat their opponents with contempt, which allowed them to engage with grace and tenacity.

Some of these elements are found in other traditions, but the combination of these principles in practice is what makes the Black Church social action tradition truly unique. As African Methodist Episcopal Zion reverend, W. H. Davenport once said, "A pound of practices is worth a ton of theological dogmas and Christian theories."[23]

They talked about morality and heaven, but unlike the White evangelical church, they didn't limit God's will in the public square to personal piety.[24] They recognized social justice as a required part of the kingdom plan. Unlike secularists, they clearly didn't interpret the separation between church and state to be a severing of one's faith from their sociopolitical engagement. Faith guided and anchored their social action.

Unlike the social gospel of today's progressive Christians, they believed the "whole counsel of God" was more than the justice imperative alone (Acts 20:27 RSV). It also involved the Bible's tenets about sin and how sin exists in all of humanity, not excluding their community or themselves. Lastly, unlike much of Black secular activism, while it understood that "power concedes nothing without a demand," they believed their social actions had to be aspirational, holy, and redemptive, and that no group of people, not even their oppressors, was irredeemable.[25] Willie Faye and Mahalia's generation were not the originators of the Black Church's social action tradition, but they were perhaps its crown. They grasped the legacy and the lessons they learned from their elders and took "bigger steps and bigger risks."[26]

This is clear in the initiative to create the Progressive National Baptist Convention. In 1961, Pastors like Dr. L. Vencheal Booth,

Dr. Martin Luther King Jr., Dr. William Augustus Jones Jr., and Dr. Gardner C. Taylor broke away from the National Baptist Convention and its elder leadership because they wanted to go further on the issue of civil rights.[27] The new denomination, led by younger pastors, maintained the orthodoxy of the NBC but wanted to further emphasize the social justice mandate as a centerpiece of their witness. The "progressive" in the name referred to its forward-looking stance on social justice, not progressive theology. They'd significantly change the race conversation, legislation, and jurisprudence dealing with race in America.[28] Historian Mary Sawyer further explains, "In the years from 1954 to 1968 . . . black churches and their pastors and members helped stage a drama that challenged the nation and captivated the world."[29]

THE ORIGINS AND SPIRIT OF THE TRADITION

While Mahalia grew up in a Baptist church, when she moved to Chicago it became clear that she'd been heavily influenced by the sound of the Black Pentecostal church a few doors from her home in New Orleans. Many of the Baptist churches in Chicago didn't appreciate the impassioned shouting and improvisation in her style.[30] Gospel singer Sallie Martin said that early on "most of the big churches still didn't receive her work . . . Some were very, very much against her—and other singers looked down their noses at her."[31] Denominationalism and classism were at play here. Many Baptists considered their music refined, unlike the frenzied shouting of lower-class Pentecostals in what was called the sanctified church.[32] But Mahalia would eventually compel some resistant Baptist audiences to "get happy" and applaud a more Pentecostal approach to worship.[33]

Mahalia would later join the choir of New Salem Baptist Church in Chicago. The music she'd create with legendary music director Thomas Dorsey would revolutionize the art form and galvanize

Black saints nationwide. Today, the Black Baptist church I attend welcomes shouting and impassioned praise, in large part based on Mahalia Jackson's legacy. She was the intoning voice of a generation of women who nurtured and powered churches, communities, and a social movement—women like Willie Faye who fed and supported the leaders before and after they preached and protested. But her voice didn't just impact the women of her time, it became the pitch for the civil rights generation in general.

If the civil rights movement had theme music and Dr. Martin Luther King Jr.'s visionary words were the bars that laced the track, then Mahalia's riveting contralto blessed the chorus, melodically expressing the ethic and motif of this world-changing social composition. She sang her signature versions of the songs "How I Got Over" and "I Been Buked and I Been Scorned" at the March on Washington in 1963 before Dr. Martin Luther King gave his famous "I Have a Dream" speech. During the speech, in the Black Church's time-honored call and response tradition, she would shout, "Tell 'em about the dream, Martin. Tell 'em about the dream."[34] That theme wasn't in his notes, and he hadn't originally intended on mentioning it that day. But Mahalia had heard Dr. King speak about "the dream" in other addresses and had experienced its power. As fate would have it, her encouragement might have catalyzed the most memorable lines of one of the greatest speeches in American history.

How often did Willie Faye and hundreds of thousands of other Black Christians in her generation find respite in Mahalia Jackson's voice? How often did they remove their soiled aprons and weathered fedoras after enduring another day of subordination and segregation and pull one of Mahalia's records from its sleeve? I imagine, almost out of necessity, they put the vinyl on the turntable, carefully placed the phonograph needle down, and through her spirituals were persuaded or even compelled to push forward another day. Or perhaps some tuned into her weekly CBS radio program, sank into the couch, or prepared soul food supper and let her powerful articulation of the sanctified gospel heal their souls.

Their pain was too real and direct for this to have simply been a routine or formulaic exercise. No, this was soul-penetrating praise and worship in the spirit of the prophet Jeremiah and King David. It was embattled petitioners saying, "LORD, hear my prayer, listen to my cry for mercy; in your faithfulness and righteousness come to my relief" (Psalm 143:1).

Through the music, we see how the spiritual and the sociopolitical were seamlessly tied together in the Black Church social action tradition. The spirituals they sang in church were the same spirituals they sang during marches and protests. In church, they'd sing about faithfully pursuing God:

> Ain't gonna let nobody turn me 'roun'
> Turn me 'roun'
> Ain't gonna let nobody turn me 'roun'
> I'm gonna wait until my change comes.

For a social action march, they might adapt the song by singing,

> Ain't gonna let no Jim Crow turn me around
> Turn me around, turn me around
> Ain't gonna let no injunction turn me around
> I'm gonna keep on a-walkin', keep on a-talkin'
> Marchin' up to freedom land.

In the same vein, the song "Keep Your Eyes on the Prize," one of the most recognizable civil rights spirituals, was an adaptation of "Keep Your Hand on the Plow," a gospel song based on Luke 9:62. Negro spirituals were ever present in the civil rights movement. It was a way for Black Christians to take the church with them as they journeyed outside the four walls of the sanctuary.

By singing spirituals in the field of life, Willie Fay and Mahalia's generation was continuing a legacy of placing God at the center of their interactions in the world. In his book *How Sweet the Sound*, Horace Clarence Boyer explains the dual role negro spirituals played in the life of slaves:

> Negro spirituals not only spoke of the slaves' relationship to God but also gave special attention to their position on earth and the difficult fate that had befallen them. The songs combined a recognition of the power of God and thanks for life, health, and strength, but more important they expressed the slaves' feelings about oppression, discrimination and the struggle to survive.[35]

For instance, the song "Didn't My Lord Deliver Daniel?" sounds like a defiant response to a cynical or hopeless statement. It speaks to God's omnipotence and reliability in dire circumstances:

> Didn't my Lord deliver Daniel, deliver Daniel, deliver Daniel?
> Didn't my Lord deliver Daniel,
> And why not a every man?
> He deliver'd Daniel from the lion's den,
> And Jonah from the belly of the whale,
> And the Hebrew children from the fi'ry furnace,
> And why not every man?

If the Lord delivered Daniel, Jonah, and the Hebrew children, then surely he was able and willing to deliver his disinherited children in America. Black Christians advocated based on that premise.

When survival and civility seemed to conflict, spirituals served as disciplines—a way of forming one's perspective and reiterating standards. From slavery to the civil rights movement, they were an immediate reminder of God's promises and commands. The songs allowed them to be present in the moment without being overcome by the moment.

Today, we see partisans beat the drums of war as they enter enemy-laden territory, but Willie Faye and Mahalia's generation sang about peace and redemptive victories as they walked across the Edmund Pettus Bridge. Gospel hymns and old-fashioned spirituals were much needed reminders of the church's foundational principles. These songs were often tirelessly repetitive, but not vainly so. They drove home the point. When your churches are bombed and your friends lynched, repeating the line "I'm gonna treat everybody right until I die" is more than just a cute lyrical phase; it's a directive to "love your neighbor as yourself" (Mark 12:31) when it's least convenient. Intently professing, "I'm going to sing til the Spirit moves in my heart, I'm going to sing til Jesus comes" isn't reciting bubblegum pop; it's surrender to the Creator and trust in his renewing power.

Faithful biblical expositions like these helped an oppressed people identify the image of God even in the most hostile manifestations of human brokenness. The only way to see human dignity in someone who hates you is to see what's invisible outside of faith. You have to want to see it and be willing to imagine it despite all other indications. You have to love and fear God too much not to see it.

Civil rights legend Fannie Lou Hamer was a model of this ethic. Hamer had been beaten until she nearly passed out under the orders of a White highway patrolman. The beating was punishment for the ghastly offense of registering Black people to vote. Years later she was asked how she felt about the offending officer. Even after being fined herself for the incident while the officer got away unpunished, Hamer was gracious. She gave a logic-defying and loving response, saying, "We have to love them and they are sick . . . America was sick and it needed a doctor and we was the hope for America."[36] This was the difference between wanting vengeance and wanting redemption even for your oppressor.

She wasn't giving the officer or American injustice a pass. She fought for justice relentlessly and sought the prosecution of the officer for his crimes. But she didn't let his behavior or the unjust system blind her to what Jesus said about even the most wicked among us: "Love your enemies and pray for those who persecute you" (Matthew 5:44).

Again, this enduring spirit and moral clarity was inherited from what the late African American religions scholar Albert Raboteau called "slave religion," where we first see the church's central role in the Black American experience. Many enslaved people were forbidden from attending church and even from praying. Yet they risked corporal punishment to attend the original Black Church, which E. Franklin Frazier called the "Invisible Institution."[37] Despite living a life of physical bondage, in the invisible institution slaves found an area where they could exercise a degree of institutional freedom. According to C. Eric Lincoln, they created a religion of their own by performing "their own rituals, songs, and other cultural forms of religious worship."[38]

They were also able develop their own leaders. Raboteau explained:

> From the abundant testimony of fugitive and freed slaves it is clear that the slave community had an extensive religious life of its own, hidden from the eyes of the master. In the secrecy of the quarters or the seclusion of the brush arbors ("hush harbors") the slaves made Christianity of their own . . . Into that all-night singing and praying the slaves poured the sufferings and needs of their days.[39]

Enslaved people didn't simply copy the faith tradition of slaveholders, "they created their own worldviews, and social and cultural institutions."[40] They interpreted the faith through a different lens. Through the Bible's exodus narrative, they identified with the suffering and the eventual liberation of the Hebrew people.[41] The God they knew and trusted was the same God that strengthened Moses and ordered him to tell Pharaoh, "Let my people go" (Exodus 8:1).

Spirituals played a key role in connecting Christianity to the experience of the enslaved community.[42] Their praise and worship were a matter of survival. C. Eric Lincoln points out, "Even a Marxist historian such as Eugene Genovese concluded . . . that slave religion played a major role in the survival of slaves."[43] Slavery is the essence of inhumanity. Such captivity, by its very nature, robs one of agency and by design arrests the development of a healthy self-image. Slaveholders often made every effort to stunt the mental and spiritual growth of the enslaved. If religion was offered to slaves, in many cases, it was a truncated gospel—void of the liberation narrative and themes that inspire hope. It was often used as an "instrument of social control."[44]

Yet, God will not be silenced by the trifles of men. The Holy Spirit still filled the hearts of those who oppression tried to keep from experiencing the fullness of God. In his slave narrative, W. L. Bost reflects on how those wicked schemes failed to keep God's word from reaching his African American slave community.

> Us [slaves] never have a chance to go to Sunday school and church. The white folks feared for [slaves] to get any religion and education, but I reckon somethin' inside just told us about God and that there was a better place hereafter.[45]

Neither the perpetuation of illiteracy nor the perversion of the biblical message was enough to mute the salvific reality of the gospel. God delivered a faithful theology to those with no formal education, while some well-educated theologians continued to endorse slavery. Just as God sent common, uneducated disciples to speak into an elitist Greco-Roman culture, God entrusted some of the lowest in America's antebellum society with a prophetic vision of his kingdom (Acts 10).

The invisible institution would become a life source and refuge where many preachers professed a theology of orthodoxy (right doctrine) and orthopraxy (right conduct). They espoused a hermeneutic of love and truth that distinguished itself from the perverted version of the faith held by slaveholders and Jim Crow endorsers. Preachers constantly reminded the shackled congregation that they were defined by God, not by institutions of oppression, and that their chains were temporal, but their freedom was inevitable. As Vince Bantu explains, "The Gospel of Jesus Christ was the cornerstone of all faith and hope for African slaves."[46]

Lincoln explained, "Historically, black churches have been the most important and dominant institutional phenomenon in African American communities."[47] It was more than just a place of worship, "but also a bulletin board to a people who owned no organs of communication . . . and even a kind of people's court." E. Franklin Frazier called the Black Church a "nation within a nation"—"the center of economic cooperation, education, and social and political life for the black community."[48] No institution invested more in the education of African Americans. Frazier goes on to say, "The Negro Church has affected the entire intellectual development and outlook of Negroes."[49]

Churchgoers in Willie Faye and Mahalia's generation greatly invested in the church and made major sacrifices for it. Some weeks, Mahalia would be exhausted after five straight nights of revival singing at Greater Salem, where all the proceeds would go to the programming for the children's ministry, "so those children wouldn't have to run around the streets."[50] Bishop Cooper and Willie Faye helped build PGT Nation Temple #1 brick by brick and paid off the last of the mortgage for Temple #2 out of their own pockets.

The Black Church's social action, at its best, was a negro spiritual in action. While the Black Church was far from unanimous in its support of social activism, "From the beginning, the civil rights movement was anchored in the Black Church."[51] Preachers and the people in the pews organized and financially supported the movement. Again, Willie Faye and Mahalia's generation of Christian advocates didn't disconnect the sacred from their engagement in the public square.

Some secular movements have interpreted religion and talk of faith and heaven as merely a form of escapism—a means of disengaging from reality. But for many the hymns helped them better engage reality. There were indeed those in their community who tried to dismiss the here and now by solely focusing on the hereafter. However, the civil rights movement was the opposite of escapism. It was an action-oriented initiative with a keen awareness of the principalities and spiritual wickedness in high places at play in society.

This supernatural perspective conflicts with the materialism of secular activism. Materialists believe only in what they can see or touch. They focus solely on the physical concerns of this world and often regard religion as a liability diverting our attention away from social change. They take God's sovereignty and providence out of the equation. The secular mind is uncomfortable with the idea of an all-powerful authority that it can't control and struggles to admit there are realities beyond human understanding. Perhaps materialism is its own form of escapism—a vain attempt to circumvent what one can't completely understand and control. Conversely, Willie Faye and Mahalia trusted God's self-disclosure, were empowered by his grace, and were at peace with the things that would only be known "by and by."

Social justice outside of the existence of a loving and just God doesn't make sense. The worldview at the center of the Black

Church's social action tradition rejected the idea that this miraculously designed world came from nothingness. A godless particle or uncreated big bang couldn't possibly create Mahalia's voice, Zora Neale Hurston's prose, George Washington Carver's scientific mind, or a slave's moral imagination. The "black sacred cosmos or the religious worldview of African Americans" saw the whole universe was sacred.[52]

Contrary to materialist narratives, acknowledging the spirit world and human limitation doesn't require a surrender to anti-intellectualism. Look no further than the brilliant Black organizers and tacticians who orchestrated the civil rights movement from church fellowship halls. Leaders like Reverend Fred Shuttlesworth strategically outwitted devious Birmingham commissioners and sheriffs, proving logic was neither scorned nor in short supply in Christian advocacy circles.[53] Great minds were at work, but those minds weren't obstacles to a greater faith. Faith and logic weren't in conflict. These believers employed both.

Ultimately, dismissing what can't fully be ascertained through the five senses is disempowering. It desensitizes us to what can be felt, captured, and achieved spiritually. They were at peace and even celebrated dependence on a higher power (Proverbs 13:4; Colossians 3:23; Hebrews 13:16). Their faith was refuge from the hopelessness of the skeptics. They also knew prayer and a song of worship could accomplish things a philosophical treatise could not.

In this chapter, I've obviously highlighted the best of the Black Church's history and prophetic public witness. However, that tradition, like any other, isn't without its warts and ongoing struggles. The truth is women often weren't given their due, certain groups were marginalized within the movement, and moral shortcomings compromised some of its leaders. As Dr. Gardner C. Taylor cautioned, "We need to reflect on the aberrations and, also some of the futile aspect of the Civil Rights Movement."[54] Notwithstanding its shortcomings, I believe the Black Church's social action tradition can provide a model for how Christian orthodoxy and orthopraxy can help the church and a polarized nation overcome the toxic culture wars and move toward a greater faithfulness and civic pluralism. Our historic public witness can correct many of the erroneous approaches, attitudes, and practices much of American Christianity has fallen into in the public square today. In other words, the Black Church has a word for this moment in the public square.

2

ON THE BATTLEFIELD

BLACK CHRISTIANS AND THE WHITE AMERICAN CULTURE WAR

I'm on the battlefield for my Lord.

E. V. Banks and Sylvanna Bell

IN A MORE IDEAL WORLD, the spirit and ethic undergirding the work of Willie Faye and Mahalia's generation would've engrossed all Christian politics and social action for generations to come. If humanity was really on one long upward journey toward progress and perfection, as philosopher Georg Hegel suggested, the lessons to be learned through their example would've surely become the standard and norm for the world to build on moving forward. If our movements were as enlightened and altruistic as we claim, the unqualified grace and self-sacrifice the world witnessed during the civil rights movement would've been permanently fixed in our ethos and modes of operation. We would've captured those virtues, improved upon their tactics, and applied them to future problems. Like the invention of the wheel, once achieved, all our social vehicles would've incorporated that advance and placed it at the center of future civic innovation. We and our social constructs would all be more forgiving and resilient than our predecessors.

Unfortunately, humanity is broken so our social relations don't quite work that way. Their gospel-centered public witness was eventually replaced by more performative and militant movements. This is because human history isn't charting one straight line to moral perfection. We don't always become more judicious and insightful than those who came before us. We do not always grow and evolve to become the moral superiors of our ancestors. Sometimes we descend and fall to lower motives. This is why King Josiah had to re-establish the word of God in Judah (2 Kings 22–23). What was once known and prominent had to be relocated and understood anew. This is why Israel repeatedly broke their covenant with God and had to repent continually (1 Kings 11:11; Isaiah 25:5; 43:21).

A similar dynamic is, in part, the reason the United States continually broke peace treaties with Native American tribes in the late 1700s and 1800s.[1] The acknowledgment of Indigenous people's right to govern themselves would eventually become an obstacle to ambitions of westward expansion. Our broken sense of self-interest sometimes clashes with the best practices we once agreed upon. Our moral knowledge doesn't always accumulate like technological data. Our collective wisdom isn't always compiled and passed down like laws of mathematics. Sometimes we misplace it or undermine it with greed and vengeance. We can, at one time, have thoughtful convictions and clear reasons for charting a more righteous path toward human flourishing. As the funk band Earth, Wind & Fire once sang in their hit "Reasons," over time "all of our reasons start to fade."

Furthermore, developments in culture and technology don't necessarily correlate with moral improvement.[2] As D. A. Carson has pointed out, Germany was thought to have the best technology, best scholarship, and best universities "at the philosophical peak of the Western Enlightenment," but their value system led to genocide during the Holocaust.[3]

Willie Faye survived on forgiveness, but decades later, her grandchildren and great grandchildren struggle to see forgiveness as anything other than weakness and docility. They "can't find the reasons."[4] We see this sentiment in the popular T-shirt with the message, "Dear Racism, I am not my ancestors, I will whoop yo ass! Unapologetically, these hands." The witty quip could be dismissed with a laugh if it wasn't coupled with a rise in politically related violent threats, harassment, and attacks.[5] Almost 20 percent of Americans somewhat or strongly agreed that "political violence against those they disagreed with was acceptable."[6] In some ways, we seem to have gone backwards.

It would be a mistake to say we've completely forgotten all the principles or don't pay homage to the movement in at least ritualistic manner. Every year on MLK Day and during Black History Month, Americans are provided with a healthy dose of civil rights movement history. Our children learn the names of these heroes, recite their speeches, and reenact their courageous deeds. The tributes and commemorative events are everywhere. We've done an excellent job of saturating the culture with civil rights movement messages and keeping the struggle at the forefront of our collective memory. The honors are well-deserved and demonstrate that America isn't completely void of moral compass. The clear consensus is the movement represents the best of America and we're all better for it. Yet, it doesn't seem to have a lasting impact on our interactions in the public square. There's an asymmetry between the ideals we commend during these times and the way we treat our political opponents.

In a way, the inspiring principles we draw from this history are treated like a relic or a dead language that we're not fully capable of or committed to resurrecting after the season is over. It's like awe-inspiring ancient garb we admire in a museum through a thick glass barrier. We examine and venerate it. We're close enough to touch it, but we'll never put it on with the same fit and purpose. The political Left and Right acknowledge its beauty, but the guiding principles have become cliché and abstract. We take the sentiment and leave the substance. We highlight the parts that serve our narratives and discard that which is inconvenient. It's enough to make us play nice for the duration of a moment of silence and then return to our toxic discourse.

We've become proficient at commercializing and co-opting the movement. Fortune 500 companies sponsor events and buy ads with plenty of civil rights platitudes, but they don't apply the movement's tenets to their business practices as they suppress wages and perpetuate income inequality. Some conservatives have found ways to make the movement serve their conveniently colorblind narrative but aren't devoted to applying the self-sacrificial mores to their immigration policies. Some progressives, on the other hand, have used the movement to launder their entire catalog of far-left agenda items while snobbishly looking down on its deep religious convictions.

As Charles Marsh explained, the New Left is never quite able to hide the "modernist conceit that what Black people do and say in church cannot possibly be taken seriously; the actions and speech of Black Christians must be recast in terms amenable to enlightened secular interests."[7] Let the ideological left tell it, the movement was more about untethered self-expression and autonomy than God and his absolute truth. But Black Christian leaders like pastor and social justice advocate Dr. Donald Parson made their perspective all too clear: "I always believed that the Bible was the truth and did not just contain the truth. I always believed in the authority of the word of God."[8]

There are those who earnestly apply the lessons and spirit of the civil rights movement to today's issues. Leaders like Bryan Stevenson of the Equal Justice Initiative and LaTasha Morrison of Be the Bridge come to mind, but in large part our most prominent movements have lost the plot and regressed in many respects. Apparently, they've found the high road to be inexpedient. They lack the grace and a commitment to neighborly self-sacrifice. Generally, they also lack the spiritual foundation, which compels us toward forgiveness, perseverance, and intellectual honesty. In sum, today's sociopolitical efforts lack the fruit of the Spirit.

For many, the cooptation of the civil rights movement might not be a consciously underhanded ploy. It's possible some of the appropriation is a product of our ability to convince ourselves that our sociopolitical team is the embodiment of the movement's virtues and principles. Perhaps we've fooled ourselves into believing that our tone and tactics meet the standards set by Willie Faye and Mahalia's generation. We're certainly capable of deceiving ourselves in that way. As Dale Carnegie famously pointed out, human nature is to blame everyone but ourselves.[9] Despite our bad behavior, we often see ourselves as well-meaning and innocent while being overcritical of others.

The most regrettable part about the present state of our political climate is no one can say, with any amount of integrity, that Christians have been a shining example amid today's chaos. We haven't distinctively been the salt and the light in the public square as of late. We're camouflaged in a political culture full of contempt and lies. Christians participated in, if not led, the attack on the United States Capitol on January 6, 2021. Some Christians unconditionally defend social movements that explicitly undermine the family and sanctity of life. Internally and externally, our public witness resembles a spawn of the world rather than an heir of the civil rights movement. Moreover, in too many instances, the American church internally reflects the disunity in American culture. We hate our brothers and sisters with differing political views with the same fervor as the world.

AN ACTS 19 RIOT MOMENT

From a cultural and political perspective, we look less like the unity of the early church in Acts 2, who "were together and had everything in common" (Acts 2:44), and more like the mob mentality politics of Acts 19. There, we see Paul's ministry interact with a variety of arenas in the public square. He testified in the synagogue, in the lecture hall of Tyrannus—an institution of higher learning—and in the streets. Interestingly, he had more success in the lecture hall than in the synagogue. The Bible says he was "arguing persuasively about the kingdom of God" (v. 8). The gospel spread throughout the province of Asia (vv. 9-10). Jews and Greeks alike were introduced to the gospel from Paul's time speaking in the academy.

Paul's incisive commentary about the weakness and insignificance of graven images disrupted the supply and demand of business economics (vv. 24-34). In other words, he interrupted the idol-trading business. In response, a wily and self-interested silversmith named Demetrius detailed how Paul's gospel-filled preaching and lectures were having an adverse impact on his business. Demetrius made shrines of the Greek goddess Artemis, the goddess of the hunt, the moon, and nature in general. He convened the craftsmen in Ephesus to address the problem Paul's message was creating for them. He reminded them how much money they made from this industry and warned them that it could all end because the apostle was going around the province telling people "gods made with human hands are no gods at all" (v. 26). Not only was their trade at risk of becoming less lucrative, but "the temple of the great goddess Artemis" would be discredited and "robbed of her divine majesty" (v. 27).

Paul must've been doing some serious preaching and professing because he clearly had these idol makers shook. The news infuriated the craftsmen and a riot ensued. Eventually, the whole city was in an uproar. Paul had to hide, as his disciples and the provincial officials begged him not to go out and publicly address the bloodthirsty crowd. The Bible says, "The assembly was in confusion: Some were shouting one thing, some another. Most of the people did not even know why they were there" (v. 32).

This is quite revealing. The riot scene shows us a large group of people full of anger and rage, but most of them couldn't even articulate why they were participating. There was a lack of purpose and direction. There wasn't likely any desire for a constructive dialogue or solutions, just a thirst for blood. Even for those who were unsure about the details of the cause, the exasperation and animosity were still coming from somewhere. Perhaps they were projecting. Maybe dreams deferred, loves lost, bills overdue, mental illness untreated, and self-medicated wounds were all being violently transferred onto an unrelated issue. The man frothing at the mouth during the January 6 insurrection, as depicted in a viral meme, was found to be suffering from serious mental health issues.[10] We also can't exclude more cynical motives and those who joined the riot just for sport like White non-residents going into inner cities to destroy property and loot during protests over racial violence.[11]

It's possible this ill-defined uproar was, for some, the natural outcry of the human condition. What does a hurting person do when they're not sure who or what to blame for their suffering? Their incoherence doesn't make the pain any less real. Whether or not we can write a thesis on our pain, we still have a deep desire to find release and make sense of our circumstances. How do hurting people express themselves when they haven't fully diagnosed the issue or identified the cure? In some cases, we just find the nearest body of enraged souls and join the chorus. In the moment, the community, however toxic, and the emotional purge can seem more important than the why behind it all. History's most effective demagogues have always been able to find a scapegoat to fill the void: "Here, my comrade, blame them and join us."

We shouldn't dismiss the plights of the rioters in Ephesus even if they expressed themselves in a misdirected and profane manner.

Some of them might've encountered serious injustices or been on the receiving end of heartbreaking misfortunes. But Paul, an itinerant preacher, wasn't likely to blame for the pain of those who were now threatening his life. His words and actions probably weren't the proximate cause of the hurt manifesting in public incivility and disgrace. Sadly, we're all liable to and probably guilty of airing out our frustrations with bad aim.

For leaders, channeling these emotions toward righteous action is much harder than kindling an explosion of rage. Providing our suffering people with a vision and purpose that inspires discipline and positivity can seem nearly impossible, but it's exactly what the leadership of the civil rights movement accomplished. Prayerfully, they edified and ordered the passions of the people, offering them cogent plans, strategies, and solutions. The gospel-centered framework of the movement provided a lens that compelled them toward redemptive social action, not just a human target to place in their crosshairs or an ensemble of off-pitch screams.

For example, in 1957, Reverend Fred Shuttlesworth resolved to enroll his daughters, Pat and Ruby, in segregated Phillips High School in Birmingham. However, when the family pulled up to the school, a White mob was determined to prevent integration.[12] They surrounded the Shuttlesworths, attacking Fred with bats and chains. The kicks and thrusts to the ground scraped most of the skin off his face and his wife was stabbed.[13] When Birmingham's Black community heard about the beating, they were understandably furious and eager to avenge their leader.

Days later, an indignant, standing-room-only crowd awaited Shuttlesworth's orders at a local church. With a head bandage and an arm sling, Shuttlesworth urged the audience to respond by redoubling their advocacy efforts, not behaving destructively. After all, he said, he was the one who'd been attacked, and if *he* wasn't going to react in anger, they shouldn't either. He responded with a grace that redeemed and reordered the tenacious fire burning within his people—a "heavenly fire." That grace kept his work righteous, and the people's tenacity disallowed cowardice and complacency in the face of evil.[14]

Looking at the chaos and confusion of America's current discourse, we appear to be in an Acts 19 riot moment in culture and politics. We've gathered in the sociopolitical arena. Some of us are shouting one expletive-ridden thing, some another expression of contempt. It often seems like the fight is dearer to us then finding the fix, and it's not clear that we always know what we're fighting for or where our behavior will lead. Our passions are strong, but our purposes are often ill-articulated and cloudy. We've identified a target for our angst and loaded all our hurts and emotional baggage onto that villain. Our opposition may very well be responsible for significant struggles in our lives, but in many cases it seems unlikely they could have caused all our problems as we're prone to suggest. We don't love our enemies, nor do we even try to display the fruit of the Spirit in the public square. We're tribal, contemptuous, and strident.

As a general proposition, the Christian public witness doesn't sound like a beautiful spiritual spreading the principles of love, peace, and truth into the public square. People who could once be described as the conscience of America can many times appear to be just another self-interested constituency willing to seize political power by any means necessary. The civil rights movement showed us that the gospel inspires us to self-sacrificially avoid hate at all costs, while simultaneously carrying out a tenacious and practical pursuit of justice through civic means.

We've failed to build on the example and foundation Willie Faye and Mahalia's generation set. If our framework hasn't been primarily shaped by the gospel, what has shaped it? What's at the root of our current perspective? Upon years of close examination in the public square, I've come to believe much of the Christian sociopolitical perspective has been molded by the culture war. Not just the culture war issues, some of which are worth contending for, but the spirit, motives, and rewards of the culture war. The culture war framework has created the same type of inarticulate, mindless, and belligerent dissension that we see at the end of Acts 19.

Regrettably, it's become the primary lens through which we view cultural and political issues. In fact, many Christians probably can't discuss the most pressing issues outside of a culture war framework. This means our worldview is more influenced by the culture war than by the gospel of Jesus Christ in some respects. But what is the culture war exactly? What are its origins and what divisions defined it?

THE HISTORY OF THE CULTURE WAR

In his 1992 address to the Republican National Convention, Pat Buchanan detailed the contours of the culture war from a conservative perspective as George H. W. Bush prepared to take on Arkansas Governor Bill Clinton in the general presidential election. His characterization of the battle at hand would ring out for decades to come.

> Ronald Reagan made us proud to be Americans again. We never felt better about our country; and we never stood taller in the eyes of the world than when the Gipper was at the helm. Mr. Clinton, however, has a different agenda. At its top is unrestricted abortion on demand . . . A militant leader of the homosexual rights movement [rose] at that [Democratic National Convention] and [said]: "Bill Clinton and Al Gore represent the most pro-lesbian and pro-gay ticket in history." And so they do . . . Bill Clinton says he supports school choice—but only for state-run schools. Parents who send their children to Christian schools, or private schools, or

> Jewish schools, or Catholic schools need not apply . . . Hillary believes that 12-year-olds should have the right to sue their parents, and Hillary has compared marriage and the family as institutions to slavery and life on an Indian reservation . . . The agenda that Clinton & Clinton would impose on America—abortion on demand, a litmus test for the Supreme Court, homosexual rights, discrimination against religious schools, women in combat units—that's change, all right. But it is not the kind of change America needs. It is not the kind of change America wants. And it is not the kind of change we can abide in a nation that we still call God's country. God bless you, and God bless America.[15]

During the same election cycle, a month earlier, New York Governor Mario Cuomo offered an alternative vision of "progress and inclusion" for America to follow, where it was conservatives who were on the wrong side of the culture war:

> Bill Clinton believes, as we all here do, in the first principle of our Democratic commitment: The politics of inclusion. The solemn obligation to create opportunities for all people . . . of whatever color, of whatever creed, of whatever sex, of whatever sexual orientation. All of them equal members of the American family . . . That is the fundamental Democratic predicate. Surrender that principle and we might as well tear the donkeys from our lapels [and] pin elephants instead. America needs Bill Clinton for yet another reason. We need a leader who will stop the Republican attempt, through laws and the courts, to tell us what God to believe in and how to apply that God's judgment to our school rooms, our bedrooms and our bodies.[16]

The faceoff both leaders were speaking into had recently been defined by American sociologist James Davison Hunter in his book aptly titled, *Culture Wars: The Struggle to Define America.* He defined the culture war as "political and social hostility rooted in different systems of moral understanding."[17] He further explained that "the contemporary culture war is ultimately a struggle over national identity—*over the meaning of America,* who we have been in the past, who we are now, and perhaps most important, who we . . . will aspire to become."[18]

It's a battle for power and cultural dominance regarding values related to family, education, art, law, and politics.[19] Hunter's work reveals the depth of America's ideological divisions with insights that still shine light on our public debate over thirty years later. The divisions may have expanded, but the lines of contention he uncovered still form the fundamental disagreements in this clash of worldviews that's had a profound impact on America institutions and how we engage one another.

The cultural conflict didn't come out of nowhere. It had been brewing for decades before it had a name. America has always had its divisions, but they weren't primarily based on ideological difference. The conflict that proceeded the culture war was drawn along denominational and doctrinal lines. For quite some time, White Protestants controlled most American institutions and pushed back fiercely against what some of them might've described as the cultural incursion of Catholic and Jewish immigrants and Mormons as well.[20] Ethnic distrust led to abuses of power by the Protestant majority. In certain jurisdictions, Catholics were unable to hold elected office, double-taxed, and generally denied religious protections.[21] Anti-Catholicism infamously led many Americans to oppose and fear the presidency of John F. Kennedy. Similarly, an influx of Jewish immigrants would face "social prejudice, and full-scale anti-Jewish violence"[22] as these Protestants felt "their world was being threatened."[23] Apparently, these outsiders needed to be trampled to make America great again.

Eventually, the rise of secularism and new faiths would incentivize an era of greater interreligious unity among traditional Judeo-Christian religions in the public square. Advances in science, criticism of the Bible, and the growth of higher education challenged the sense of morality they shared. The primary conflict would go from "theological or doctrinal disagreements" to more fundamental disputes about the "sources of moral truth" with traditionalists on one side and progressivists on the other.[24]

While these traditionalist religions had serious quarrels, they shared a belief that truth came from one God who, as Creator, ruled sovereignly over humanity by way of scriptural commands. Their differences began to seem smaller when that conclusion was challenged by a more secular value system coming out of Europe. The Western philosophy of rationalism taught that human reason was the path to all knowledge and truth rather than religious dogma.[25] Later, Swiss-born thinker Jean-Jacques Rousseau would shift the focus of truth to the individual's inner feelings and contend that collective norms (including religious tenets) were the enemy of individual freedom. Rousseau would say, "Man is born free, yet everywhere he is in chains."[26] Humanity needed to be freed from the moral constraints of society to reach its potential and fulfillment as individuals.

What traditionalists saw as higher authority ordering man and society for the good of all, this emerging system of belief believed to be social constructs oppressing the individual. German philosopher Friedrich Nietzsche would come along and assert there were no facts or universal truth that applied to everyone, there were only interpretations.[27] He rejected all moral authority in favor of autonomy—a morality created and approved by the individual themselves. Austrian neurologist Sigmund Freud placed the expression of sexual desire at the center of the human pursuit of happiness.[28] A compilation and expansion of all these philosophies was at the root of the cultural progressivism that was challenging the old Judeo-Christian consensus.

In sum, the heart of this dispute was about moral authority, knowledge, and truth. Traditionalists taught that truth was derived from an all-powerful and all-knowing God, who disclosed himself through the Torah or the Christian Bible and who had ultimate authority. This conception of truth was timeless and applied to everyone without regard for individual opinions or tendencies. Human reason and feelings didn't dictate what was morally true. If God said homosexual behavior was wrong, then one's same-sex attraction or differing opinion based on their thoughts or experiences didn't justify it. What was truly right and wrong was established outside of humanity by God's Word and design.

Conversely, in cultural progressivism, moral authority and truth were not determined outside of humanity. They were not to be imposed on us by age-old mores from an authority reigning over us. What was right and wrong was discovered through the evolving beliefs and ideas of the day, by advances in human reason, and by the conclusions drawn from individual feelings and experience. Consequently, even if the Torah says homosexuality is wrong, the enlightened age could correct that notion and each individual's subjective experience and preferred mode of expression could determine that same-sex sexual behavior was right for them. Progressivism was presenting a completely different understanding of the world and it was beginning to win converts in American society. It generally rejected the idea of individual sin.

The progressive movement wasn't only occurring outside of the church and synagogue. There was a shift to the left happening inside those institutions as well. Intellectual elites in all those traditions were influenced by the Enlightenment and other European scholarship to deemphasize the supernatural and focus exclusively on ethical aspects of the respective religions.[29] They wanted the church to focus less on biblical concepts they found inconvenient or hard to believe and more on social issues and becoming acceptable to the modern world.

J. Gresham Machen confronted this reality in his book *Christianity and Liberalism* as more progressive theology began to penetrate Christian institutions. A Princeton-trained scholar, he believed Christianity was being attacked "from within by a movement which is anti-Christian to the core."[30] Machen argued that Christianity without miracles and doctrine was not Christianity at all.

> It may appear that what the liberal theologian has retained after abandoning to the enemy one Christian doctrine after another is not Christianity at all, but a religion which is so entirely different from Christianity as to belong in a distinct category. Modern liberalism may be criticized (1) on the ground that it is un-Christian and (2) on the ground that it is unscientific.[31]

Here, "liberal" and "progressive" could be used almost interchangeably. Machen's argument would not win the day within the institutions he was a part of. He would be ex-communicated from Presbyterian Church (USA) and he withdrew from his professorship at Princeton Seminary. He'd go on to found the Orthodox Presbyterian Church and Westminster Seminary.[32] While traditionalists today have been known for their overreactions, the struggles of orthodox leaders like Machen in the 1920s and 1930s prove the threats of their time were far from imaginary. Catholic and Jewish institutions experienced similar institutional pressures.

This forced what Hunter called a "new ecumenism"—"special purpose organizations whose explicit aim is to formally bind together the orthodox of different faiths or the progressives of different faiths to oppose coalitions on the other side."[33] A practical truce was formed for cultural and political purposes once what was perceived as a greater threat arose. In the '60s and '70s, secular progressive movements and the worldview in general started to assert themselves in popular culture with a vengeance. The sexual revolution started leaking—or better yet flooding—from the margins into the mainstream of America. As their philosophical forefathers declared, it was time for the repression of the autonomous self to end.

Sociologist Tom W. Smith defined the sexual revolution as "a revolutionary uprooting of traditional sexual morality . . . It has prompted the avant garde to celebrate the overthrow of a repressive Puritanism and traditionalists to lament the triumph of libertine hedonism."[34] Some conservatives have placed the advent of birth control at the center of the emergence of the sexual revolution since it "allowed women to separate sex from procreation."[35] The Food and Drug Administration approved the first oral contraception in 1960.[36] Within two years, 1.2 million women were using the Pill.[37] Other scholars believe the sexual revolution started during World War II.[38] Either way, during the coming years, openness about promiscuous sexuality and drug use were on the rise, and media was in the middle of it all. Eric Schaefer said, "The sexual revolution was a media revolution."[39]

Commentary on this new phenomenon was all over newspapers and magazines, as they "covered the Pill and promiscuity, rising hemlines and venereal disease, coed dorms and sex on campus, and singles bars and open marriages."[40] Sexually explicit books like Jacqueline Susann's *Valley of the Dolls* and sexually explicit movies like Vilgot Sjöman's *I Am Curious (Yellow)* were entertainment for more and more Americans.[41] Television shows like *The Love Boat* and *The Dating Game* brought sexual innuendo into American family rooms on a regular basis.

Of course, music from Elvis Presley to Serge Gainsbourg and Jane Birkin was always pushing the limits of decency.[42] Sexually suggestive music was becoming pop music. Simultaneously, LGBT movements were asserting themselves in the streets. Gays and lesbians rioted in Greenwich Village, New York, during the Stonewall Uprising signaling their empowerment and a new resistance. The seminal case *Roe v. Wade* passed in 1973 giving women the right to have an abortion and setting a new battle ground for decades to come. The US Office of Education started funding training for sex education teachers, and porn was also on the rise.[43]

This "blitzkrieg of social change" was a sure sign of America's moral decline in the eyes of traditionalists, and a televangelist turned political leader would use it to motivate a new rightwing movement. In 1979, Reverend Jerry Falwell founded the Moral Majority to save America from what he and his circle believed was the threat of a hedonistic redefinition of America. Under the banner of "family values," the religious right would galvanize evangelical Christians all over the country to influence national elections and legislation through voter registration, lobbying, and fundraising.[44] They'd become a most crucial voting block for Ronald Reagan's brand of conservatism[45] as they fought vigorously against abortion (originally a Catholic issue), homosexuality, sex education, pornography, and in support of prayer in schools, among other things.

The Moral Majority became incredibly efficient at mobilizing White evangelicals, who had been hesitant about partisan politics, to engage and fight against the New Left's cultural onslaught.[46] In the spirit of new ecumenism or practicality, they included traditionalist Catholics, Jews, and Mormons.[47] Their pro-family and pro-America branding was backed by a tenacious, if not cruelly sharp-elbowed approach to civic engagement. The culture war would be treated like a zero-sum war of worlds, where mercy and civic pluralism were essentially pejoratives. The charity and neighborly compassion of Jesus Christ would have to be laid aside for wartime measures. The battle lines were drawn. The soldiers had closed ranks and were marching toward a decades long and still ongoing battle for control of the values and norms of America.

As you might've noticed, what's missing from this equation are the views and influences of racial minorities, which is one of several major problems with this dynamic. The lack of color in the history of the culture war is glaring. This battle of worldviews was led and framed almost exclusively by dueling sides of White America. Hunter confirms this point by explaining that the culture war took place primarily within sectors of White America.[48] It was a fight between White conservatives and White progressives.

Black and Brown people certainly cared and had strong opinions about some of the issues being debated, but we, in large part, were not factored into the overall back and forth. We might've been used for optics or as pawns from time to time, but the culture war certainly didn't reflect how the primary stream of the Black Church approached many of these questions. The rejection of absolute truth on the Left and the rejection of social justice and difference on the Right were both counter to the Black Church's understanding of justice and morality. The minorities whose voices were platformed were often coming out of or representing White institutions.

Decades later, More in Common's "Hidden Tribes" study confirmed that the same two demographics are still controlling America's discourse. The data from this project revealed "Progressive Activists" and "Devoted Conservatives," the two most extreme categories, who are 8 percent and 6 percent of the American population respectively, have maintained an outsized voice in the public square. The two groups can't seem to agree on anything, but they have two important things in common: they're rich and White. The study notes, "It often feels as if our national conversation has become a shouting match between these two groups."[49]

To a large extent, the Moral Majority came from the same tradition that opposed the civil rights movement, so the Black Church was, generally, not on great terms with their coalition. As Dr. Martin Luther King Jr. once said, "In the midst of blatant injustices inflicted upon the Negro, I have watched white churchmen stand on the sideline and mouth pious irrelevancies and sanctimonious trivialities."[50] The sexual revolution got White evangelicals out of their seats in a way civil rights never did. The traditional Black Church shared many of the Moral Majority's theological pieties, but they would not be a significant part of the coalition. Theologian Andrew Martin highlighted that Black social preaching refused the "binary choices between theological liberalism and evangelicalism or social liberalism and conservativism."[51]

The Black Church was also far from celebrating the New Left's penchant for hedonism. Pastor and justice advocate Dr. Gardner C. Taylor, who was known as the "Dean of Preachers," spoke on the error of elites in the academy dismissing sin. He said they may think sin is an "old, outworn notion," but "the consequences of sin are not outworn . . . I speak of broken families, war, and overdoses. The consequences of sin live on!"

In a sermon titled "Why Modern Man Needs the Gospel," Taylor would warn about humans making themselves the arbiters of truth and separating from religion:

> Modern man! Transplanter of human organs! Voyager to the immensities of outer space . . . master of government, architect of his own destiny, master of his fate, and captain of his soul. What pride we have in ourselves! We need no supernatural help, for we ourselves are as gods and we find the right answers in our own wisdom. [But] When the sense of God goes, all that is worthwhile in society goes also. Freed from the restraints of religion, the passions rush forth like mad demons to disfigure and scar all of life.[52]

According to historian Mary Beth S. Mathews, African American Christians deliberately refused to entirely side with the Left or the Right in the culture war. They refused to sacrifice social justice to appease conservatives or undermine the Bible as the source of truth to align with liberals/progressives.[53] Historian Mary R. Sawyer has detailed "the both/and nature of African American Protestantism," which was at odds with the culture war's false dichotomy between social justice and personal piety.[54]

In her book *Doctrine and Race*, Mathews further explains that "the terms liberal and conservative are too binary to be of assistance" in trying to understand the Black Church's theological and political positions. She framed it by saying they "embraced a traditional stand on religion and a progressive stand on race relations."[55] These positions were "carefully considered and allowed them to remain true to their faith while advancing social justice."[56] Other prominent Black movements that had strong theological and philosophical disagreements with the Black Church, like the Nation of Islam and the Black Panthers, also opposed many of the Left's core beliefs.

Some progressive writers, like Andrew Hartman, have tried to cut and paste Black people onto the left side of culture war history.[57] That idea might boost the Left's narrative, but it's ultimately, intellectually dishonest and revisionist. It's a product of the White progressive cooptation and issue laundering discussed earlier. Even when Black movements and White progressive movements were pushing back against the same power structure, their values and approaches were different. Sociologist Seymour Martin Lipset noted the difference between Black and White college activists in the late 1960s:

> Black student protest differs considerably from that of the more affluent white radicals in that the politics of the former is much more instrumental, directed toward realistic, achievable goals, whereas that of the latter is inclined to be

> expressive, more oriented toward showing up the immorality of the larger society than to securing attainable reforms.[58]

While Black movements certainly fought vigorously against aspects of conservative politics, their view of what constituted liberation was fundamentally different than the cultural left too. For instance, they didn't have "hippie privilege." Hippies had the luxury of "creating artificial marginality" and they "had less at stake than those fighting for civil rights" so they could cosplay rather than engaging as a matter of survival.[59] Their extremely performative antics could seem like adolescent rebellion.

There may have been some Black academics who were defining liberation based on Western European terms of self-expression and sexuality, but that was hardly the Black perspective on the ground. Even outside the Black Church, groups like the Nation of Islam and the Black Power Movement, were not fighting for a liberation based on terms of the hippy counterculture movement. The Black Muslim critique of White progressives was just as sharp as their critique of White conservatives. Malcolm X called White conservatives "the wolf" and White liberals "the fox" for what he saw as different approaches to predatory behavior. The wolf showed its teeth—its bad intentions were explicit and unhidden. Conversely, the fox was sly and deceptive. It hid its malicious motives and often posed as a friend.

Hartman cites Black Panther Eldridge Cleaver's book *Soul on Ice* but doesn't mention his harsh critique of what he saw as the emasculation of Black men by progressivism and white supremacy.[60] It's fair to say that not all Cleaver's thoughts about gender and sexuality were compassionate and healthy. Be that as it may, what was likely the most well-known book written by a Black Panther certainly wasn't in line with the feminist and sexuality politics of the White progressive or conservative movements of the time.

The White progressive worldview simply wasn't the same lens through which these movements saw the issues. Just like enslaved people didn't merely echo the culture and worldview of slaveholders, Black movements didn't mirror the causes of their White progressive contemporaries. They had their own "bag" and values that often saw sexuality, masculinity, and individual autonomy much differently.

This likely explains why, in 2008, many of the same Black Californians who voted for Barack Obama for president also supported Proposition 8, a referendum defining marriage as the union of one man and one woman.[61] The national media was stunned. When NBC News asked a Black Christian woman why she supported the ballot initiative, she said:

> I think it's mainly because of the way we were brought up in the church; we don't agree with it. I'm not really the type that I wanted to stop people's rights. But I still have my beliefs, and if I can vote my beliefs that's what I'm going to do. God doesn't approve it, so I don't approve it. And I approve of Him.[62]

The culture war is a social and political battle between White conservatives and progressives for the norms and values of America. While Black Christians opined on these issues from time to time, we were never principals in the dispute.

The Black Church tradition wasn't fighting for cultural supremacy, as Congressman and Pastor Richard Cain explained. They demanded the rights bestowed upon them by God and upheld by the Constitution:

> We plead conscientiously before God, believing that these are our rights by inheritance, and by the inexorable decree of Almighty God.
>
> We believe in the Declaration of Independence, that all men are born free and equal, and are endowed by their Creator with certain inalienable rights.[63]

Nevertheless, we've been greatly impacted by the outcomes of this battle. How could the culture war have been different if both sides embraced the principles and disciplines espoused by Wille Fay and Mahalia's generation during the civil rights movement? How could the moral imagination supplied by a Christian faith have led those who disagreed to view each other differently, with respect and intellectual humility?

While our lives are significantly impacted by the culture war inputs and outcomes—the laws, cultural mores, and incessant fighting—Black people have never been the principal or had any type of leading authority in this battle.

3

A WRETCH LIKE ME

HOW WE VIEW OTHERS AND OURSELVES

ONE THING WILLIE FAYE'S CHILDREN and grandchildren knew not to do around her was use the word *hate*. Saying you hated someone in front of my grandmother was the equivalent of cussing and it would be addressed swiftly and sternly. Even if we were joking, we'd be admonished and reminded about what the Bible had to say about hate: "Whoever claims to love God yet hates a brother or sister is a liar. For whoever does not love their brother and sister, whom they have seen, cannot love God, whom they have not seen" (1 John 4:20). The word *hate* was nothing to play with. Among Willie Faye and Mahalia's generation, the prohibition on hate was just as important, if not more important, than the command to do justice.

When Fannie Lou Hamer was asked why she didn't even hate Southern segregationists she said, "Ain't no such a thing as I can hate anybody and hope to see God's face."[1] They knew that hate destroyed the hater internally, even if they had been victimized. Hate is a disease that makes us spiritually sick. Hamer would also say, "Hate won't only destroy us. It will destroy these people that's hating as well." No amount of wrongdoing justified hatred because it's an offense against God. It's a denial of the *imago Dei.*

Again, Christians must see the image of God in the ugliest manifestations of human brokenness. The Black Church social action tradition shows us it's possible. Black people were being denied the right to vote, spat upon, and lynched, yet they had the moral knowledge to understand that reciprocating hatred would distance them from God. It's one thing to talk about this principle in the abstract, it's quite another thing to employ it during tragedy, but the Black Church has done both. In 2015, a twenty-one-year-old white supremacist Dylann Roof entered Mother Emanuel AME Church, a Black Church in Charleston, South Carolina, during Bible-study. He was welcomed in by the congregants.[2] However, he would later draw a gun and take the lives of nine of the Black people in the church.[3]

The collective response of the victims' families shocked the nation. At Roof's sentencing hearing, the church and family members explicitly forgave him. Some publicly stated their opposition to the death penalty. *The Washington Post* reported, "One by one, those who chose to speak at a bond hearing did not turn to anger. Instead, while he remained impassive, they offered him forgiveness and said they were praying for his soul, even as they described the pain of their losses." One victim's sister sorrowfully explained, "I acknowledge that I am very angry . . . But one thing [my sister] always enjoined in our family . . . is she taught me that we are the family that love built. We have no room for hating, so we have to forgive. I pray God on your soul."[4]

To pray for Dylann Roof's soul after his monstrous act and his refusal to repent or apologize demonstrates a keen understanding of the implications of all people bearing the image of God. It means our human dignity is innate, it isn't based on our behavior. Not even Roof could render himself irredeemable or fully erase the mark of God from his life. He deserved to be punished, but Christian principles said he couldn't be held in utter contempt, nor could his actions be allowed to set the standard. Conversely, the culture war is fueled by hatred and contempt. It's created a bottomless pit of ever-descending standards on several accounts.

Major crises are impacted by how we view each other through a culture war lens. For instance, the Reagan administration was negligently slow in responding to the AIDS epidemic, at times even laughing it off in press conferences as a "gay plague."[5] Sadly, many Christians followed suit. It's fair to assume the Reagan administration's response would have been different if the disease was ravaging a demographic like suburban moms. It's possible their base's views of the gay community caused them to treat this devastating issue with less consideration and concern. Almost a million people have died from HIV-related illnesses in America.[6] All the blame certainly can't be placed on the administration, but their lack of effort is appalling. We can't correct those failures if the subject isn't a part of the public discourse.

As unpleasant and dead-ended as the culture war back and forth might appear, running away from culture war debates isn't a sensible or realistic option. In a pluralistic society, where people have drastically different beliefs on life-or-death questions, these discussions are unavoidable. Asking someone not to care about what their children are learning in sex education class or if their marriage will be recognized in certain states is unserious. Many culture war issues must be addressed. The question isn't whether these issues need to be addressed, but how we see and value each other within the debate. Do we see our cultural and political opposition as image bearers or an irredeemable "basket of deplorables"?[7]

THE FRAMEWORK—GOOD VS. EVIL

In Luke 18, Jesus told a parable about a religious man, a Pharisee, who offered up to God an earnest prayer that unfortunately, demonstrated an over-confidence in his own righteousness. The man said, "God, I thank you that I am not like other people—robbers, evildoers, adulterers—or even like this tax collector. I fast twice a week and give a tenth of all I get" (vv. 11-12). On the other hand, the tax collector, whom the religious man had just condemned, approached God with a sense of humility, need, and dependence. The scorned man was too remorseful to even look up. He pounded his chest and prayed, "God, have mercy on me, a sinner" (v. 13). Jesus said the second man "went home justified before God" because he humbled himself instead of exalting himself (v. 14).

The religious man was right about the tax collector's disreputable function in society. At the time, tax collectors charged tolls and collected tax revenue from the Jewish people for the Roman government. They were often unethical and known for overcharging for personal profit. Because of their willingness to participate in the oppressive Roman system, they were hated among their own people.

According to Bible scholar Jeffrey E. Miller,

> Since the Jews considered themselves victims of Roman oppression, Jewish tax collectors who overtaxed their fellow countrymen were especially despised. Jews viewed such favor for Rome as betrayal and equal to treason against God. Rabbinic sources consistently align Jewish tax collectors with robbers.[8]

Furthermore, Jewish leaders regarded tax collectors as ceremonially unclean and excluded them from religious activities. Jesus acknowledged the ill-repute of tax collectors in other parables as well (Matthew 21:31-32). Accordingly, the religious leader was possibly right in his assessment about the publican's negative social impact outweighing his own, but he's wrong on other more important accounts. First, he failed to recognize that he was also a sinner in need of God's grace. He suggests his works and his point of view rendered him good and morally superior to his list of sinners. His fasting and tithing had not made him righteous. If he had any righteousness in him, it was on account of God and shouldn't lead to this type of self-exaltation.

Second, he was looking down on others. His prayer was self-righteous and prideful. He felt morally accomplished in comparison to "robbers, evildoers, adulterers," and tax collectors, as if the standard for righteousness was set by some sort of human median. Those above the median, based on their actions, opinions, and social impact would be found righteous. Those below it were to be condemned. However, that's not how it works out in God's economy. Jesus explicitly rejects the religious leader's calculus by saying the tax collector would be exalted in his humility unlike the religious leader who would be humbled in his pride. The true standard of righteousness is faith—the faith of those who know they are unworthy of God's grace and know God is the only source of righteousness, not our works (Romans 1:17; 2 Corinthians 5:21; Isaiah 64:6). Our social impact is not unimportant, but it is certainly insufficient. This principle is of great important in relation to how we view others and view ourselves in comparison.

In the Old Testament, the prophet Jonah ran into a similar issue because of his contempt for the people in Nineveh. Nineveh was a large heathen city in Assyria and a longtime enemy of Israel.[9] The first time God told Jonah to minister to the Ninevites he refused and ran away. Jonah would rather die than see this wicked group of people receive God's grace (Jonah 1:12). After a wild journey through the sea and the belly of a whale, Jonah finally agrees to half-heartedly prophesy in Nineveh. Despite his lackluster effort, the people repent and Jonah is upset with God because of the breadth and width of his mercy.

Both the religious leader in Luke 18 and Jonah drew a line between themselves and others that they believed distinguished good from evil. The culture war mirrors this good-versus-evil narrative. The stories and symbols of both sides creatively, if not by self-deception, present their disagreements as a battle between those with positive intentions and those with negative intentions. This isn't a gospel-centered view of the world. It actually more closely resembles the heresy Manicheanism, which many Christians have fought against historically because it sought salvation through special knowledge that made certain people good.[10]

Social scientist and Harvard professor Arthur Brooks discusses this dynamic in his book *Love Your Enemies* based on a phenomenon called "motive asymmetry." This perspective assumes our side is purely motivated by love, while our opponents are motivated by malice. Brooks says, "The two sides think that they are driven by benevolence while the other side is evil and motivated by hate."[11] This is a product of human pride that makes for a clean and tight narrative by which to prosecute our case in the public square. The problem is that it's not an accurate depiction of reality.

Charles Taylor also examines this tendency in *A Secular Age*:

> We fight against injustices which cry out to heaven for vengeance. We are moved by a flaming indignation against these: racism, oppression, sexism or leftist attacks on family or Christian faith . . . [This is] fed by our sense of superiority that we are not like these instruments and accomplices of evil . . . Our picture of the world has safely located all evil outside of us.[12]

Recognition of the impurity of all motivations kept Willie Faye and Mahalia's generation focused on the cultivation of both sanctified ends and sanctified means to those ends. No one expressed this better than Martin Luther King in a speech entitled, "Facing the Challenge of a New Age."

> The end is reconciliation; the end is redemption; the end is the creation of the beloved community. It is this type of spirit and this type of love that can transform opposers into friends.

> It is this type of understanding good that will transform the deep gloom of the old age into the exuberant gladness of the new age. It is this love which will bring about miracles in the hearts of men.[13]

This isn't an endorsement of relativism—the idea that there's no absolute truth and, therefore, what's right and wrong is a matter of opinion or is dependent upon the situation. The tax collector was wrong for corruptly overtaxing the people in any age during any day of the week. The Ninevites were wrong for their immoral ways in all contexts and time periods. To the contrary, as King's speech indicates, it trains our attention on the good that we seek and the means required to achieve it rather than on demonization of our opponents as the unrighteous.

This also isn't a romantic false equivalence. The Bible doesn't force us to pretend some people's behavior isn't far worse than others. In fact, Jonah was sent by God to call out Nineveh's wrongdoing and Jesus spoke on the unrighteousness of the tax collectors. The Bible tells us to expose evil: "Have nothing to do with the fruitless deeds of darkness, but rather expose them" (Ephesians 5:11). Accordingly, it's unfaithful for us to observe evil and not bear witness against it.

After a Black man was stopped by a police officer for speeding in Montgomery and beaten nearly to death with a tire iron, Vernon Johns, Martin Luther King's predecessor at Dexter Avenue Baptist, announced on the church's marquee the title of his next sermon, "It's Safe to Murder Negroes in Montgomery." When called before a judge to explain himself, Johns calmly gave a brief address of the suppression of free speech, and when the judge asked why anyone would want to preach on a subject so inflammatory, Johns responded, "Because everywhere I go in the South the Negro is forced to choose between his hide and his soul . . . Mostly, he chooses his hide. I'm going to tell him that this hide is not worth it."[14]

Discerning right from wrong was not where these two men erred. Their mistake was not in condemning immoral actions but in condemning people while exalting themselves. They assumed the line between good and evil is what separated them from those they judged. They spoke as if they were completely pure and the other group was inherently corrupt, but that's never the case. We all have the potential to do serious evil if left to our own devices. Aleksandr Solzhenitsyn, a political prisoner during Joseph's Stalin's regime put it this way:

> The line separating good and evil passes not through states, nor between classes, nor between political parties either—but right through every human heart—and through all human hearts. This line shifts. Inside us, it oscillates with the years. And even within hearts overwhelmed by evil, one small bridgehead of good is retained.[15]

There is good and evil, but social groups don't fall neatly to one side or the other.

Because of her faith, Fannie Lou Hamer survived the Jim Crow South seeing White Southerners the same way Jonah saw Ninevites. She said she felt sorry for a patrolman who almost had her beaten to death. She also urged others to love him and described him as sick instead of condemning him as irredeemable.[16] In explaining how the coalition to improve housing for African Americans in Chicago proceeded in implementing the beloved community in the mid-1960s, Bernard Lafayette Jr. wrote the following:

> Even though you recognize, for example, systematic forms of discrimination or efforts to deny people equality, you work to change these conditions and these attitudes and you refuse to hate. You exemplify the attitude of forgiveness, putting love into action. Your behavior exemplifies what you expect in return.[17]

A BETTER FRAMEWORK: *IMAGO DEI* AND ORIGINAL SIN TENSION

We must change frameworks to better understand this concept. We can't see humanity as engaged in a battle of good versus evil with some social groups on one side and some on the other. Rather we should see humanity through the tension between *imago Dei* and original sin. In her book *Nannie Helen Burroughs: A Documentary Portrait of an Early Civil Rights Pioneer*, scholar Kelisha Graves explained that Burroughs, a Black Christian woman (who'll be analyzed in more detail later in the book), based her "prophetic principle of human equality on two theological truths:

1. All human beings are equal because we are made in the image of God;
2. All human beings are equal because 'we are all sinners before God.'"[18]

The concept of *imago Dei* appears in the book of Genesis multiple times (Genesis 1:27; Genesis 5:1-3; Genesis 9:6). It's a Latin phrase meaning humans were created in the "image of God."[19] Genesis 1:27 says, "So God created mankind in his own image, in the image of God he created them." Since all of humanity is made in the image of God, we have an innate value. This is the basis of human dignity, inalienable human rights, and social justice.[20] We all have eternal worth and as a result we must always be treated up to a certain standard. When we don't acknowledge the human dignity in others, we sin against God by violating his likeness in them. In the New Testament *imago Dei* is used as part of the Christian's responsibility to imitate Christ.[21]

This is why we're commanded to love not only those who love us but also our enemies (Matthew 5:43-48). We're told we can't truly love God if we don't love others as ourselves. No matter how unrighteous their behavior, we must realize they're deserving of our consideration. This isn't about giving those who abuse others a pass. They're still responsible for their actions and subject to punishment in proportion to their wrongdoing, as are we. However, the *imago Dei* sets limits to how negatively we can think about others and how harshly we can treat even the worst offenders. We must speak piercing truth to power, but we've gone too far once we suggest they're not worthy of grace.

Before Jesus' final breath, he even had mercy on those who crucified him: "Father, forgive them, for they do not know what they are doing" (Luke 23:34). His example shows us their value, redeemability, and that they could have something to contribute to humanity. We glorify God when we're able to acknowledge the human dignity of those who wrong us. Seeing God in otherwise wretched people opens our eyes to their potential, redeemability, and their pain. It's a matter of moral imagination.

The *imago Dei* is in tension with original sin. We're made in the image of God, but we've been compromised by sin. The *imago Dei* prevents us from looking down on others. Original sin prevents us from exalting ourselves. The *imago Dei* is the reason Fannie Lou Hamer loved those who persecuted her. Original sin is the sickness she referred to in those who mistreated her. Hamer's diagnosis of the racist patrolman as sin sick rather than purely evil was an insightful biblical exposition. It allowed her to separate his actions from the essence of his humanity enough to feel sympathy and love.

Much of the problem with the culture war framework comes down to how we see others, especially our opponents, and how we see ourselves in comparison. Where the culture war perpetuates and manipulates the good-versus-evil narrative, the gospel of Jesus Christ forces Christians to reckon with the sin in us and God's image in our opposition no matter how hidden. We can't in good faith see ourselves as all good or any other group and irredeemably evil. Choosing the good-versus-evil narrative over the *imago Dei*/

original sin tension has dire consequences. When you've concluded that your ideological opposition is completely evil, nothing they do can be right and no measure taken to thwart them is excessive. As James Davison Hunter observed, "Culture wars always precede shooting wars. They don't *necessarily* lead to a shooting war, but you never have a shooting war without a culture war prior to it, because culture provides the justifications for violence."[22]

NEIGHBORS AND ADVOCATES

In his famous "Letter from a Birmingham Jail," Dr. King said, "We are caught in an inescapable network of mutuality, tied in a single garment of destiny."[23] He was explaining that the destinies of all Americans, regardless of their color or class, were tied together whether we liked it or not. If one group is forced to endure injustice, it stains the entire country. Where the culture war positions us as separate groups fighting to dominate and extinguish others, the gospel shows us the insufficiency of love that's limited to our in-group. In Luke 6:32-33, Jesus explains, "If you love those who love you, what credit is that to you? Even sinners love those who love them. And if you do good to those who are good to you, what credit is that to you? Even sinners do that." The gospel raises the standard of how we should view and treat our enemies far past what the world can logically justify. In earnestly dealing with our own brokenness, we're forced to show grace to others even when their perspectives and behavior harm us. We can hold people accountable and give them the grace they don't deserve because of the undeserved grace we've received.

In Luke 10, after reciting the Great Commandment, a lawyer asks Jesus, "And who is my neighbor" (v. 29). Here, the word *neighbor* implied nearness, community, and fellowship, which one could conveniently interpret as being exclusive to Israelites or those who upheld similar theological beliefs.[24] Surely, they would be able to exclude Gentiles and Herodians. Through the Good Samaritan parable, Jesus shows the lawyer that neighbor extends to humanity in general (vv. 30-36). We should love and feel a nearness toward them because of the *imago Dei.* The lawyer wanted to get technical, but God requires a change of heart. He doesn't allow us to manipulate technicalities to avoid divine principles.

The culture war lures us into asking similar questions. Who is on our side or who is in our tribe? Who do I have to show compassion to? Who can I exclude based on their ideology, political party, identity, or behavior? Once we can exclude certain groups from the neighbor category, our attitudes and behavior toward them can fall below the standards of human dignity.

We see this dynamic in Exodus 1. When Joseph was alive, the Hebrew people were treated well. They had been welcomed into Egypt during the famine and allowed to settle in "the best part of the land" (Genesis 47:8-12) where they were fruitful and multiplied (Exodus 1:6-7). But when Joseph died, a new king to whom Joseph meant nothing stepped in. From his perspective, the growth of the Hebrews was a threat and would lead to future problems.

He didn't see the destinies of the Egyptians and the Hebrews as being tied together in a network of mutuality. By telling his people they needed to treat the Hebrews harshly, Pharaoh was severing any sense of connectedness and community between the two groups. Joseph's people were now merely political abstractions or markers on a war room strategy map. In sum, the Hebrews were no longer seen as neighbors. They were once again viewed as outsiders whose flourishing wasn't an asset to Egypt but a liability.

This point of view opened the door to oppression through slavery. It justified treating the Hebrews bitterly with harsh labor because, according to Pharaoh's narrative, their prosperity stood in the way of Egyptian prosperity (Exodus 1:10-14). And to some extent, this is how we see our cultural and political opposition in the culture war—as people to be defeated and treated harshly. We pretend our nation would be nearly perfect if we could just make all those conservatives or progressives disappear. It's the same root of detachment, self-interest, and contempt Pharaoh had planted in his people. Leaders like Marjorie Taylor Green have even called for a national divorce that would separate the country by red and blue states.

THE TYRANT IMPULSE

When we read Exodus, we do so from the perspective of the Hebrews, but I'd submit that we all have some Pharaoh in us. And the more we ignore it, the more we risk our power becoming our condemnation; the more our arrogance can turn us into exactly what we think we're fighting against.

I call it the "Tyrant Impulse." The temptation in every group and in every movement to silence or erase others, to unduly prevent them from pursuing different cultural or political ends. It's the urge not to win the debate, but to summarily end the debate through intimidation or force. The tyrant is usually thought of as an individual authoritarian, but it can also be a collective ideological tyrant, which urges the state to do its bidding and punish its enemies.

Those acting on the Tyrant Impulse can't tolerate political, social, or cultural disagreement. Our ideologies can be tyrannical when they convince us we're so right that we shouldn't have to explain ourselves or endure opposition. They blind us to the potential intellectual and moral merits on the other side. We start to believe narratives like all gun control advocates are part of a conspiracy to leave the average American defenseless or all pro-life advocates just want to control women's bodies. In our brokenness, the impulse is in all of us. The question is whether we act on it.

Those who don't deliberately extinguish the Tyrant Impulse in their camp are bound to succumb to it. They rarely see themselves for what they've become, especially if they're upholding what they've honestly deemed to be a good cause. We tend to think pursuing a good cause means we're doing good, but that's not necessarily the case. A good cause has never guaranteed ethical means and righteous conclusions. Like the way a medication that's meant to ease pain can become the center of an epidemic of addiction, a good cause can end in iniquity. Further, it's a misreading of history to say that what all tyrants have in common is an obviously malicious cause. Some do, but it's not the common denominator. Some tyrants have championed what were initially good causes. It can be argued that Joseph Stalin started with legitimate concerns about the injustice of the ruling class, but his initial cause didn't prevent him from doing great evil.

What's common among all tyrants is not equal malevolence of cause, but the willingness to violate the human dignity of others to achieve their objectives. It's also the willingness to promote narratives that make other groups appear to lack value and be unworthy of respect. They share a desire to crush institutions that amplify the voice and agency of others. Under the influence of the Tyrant Impulse, we can't simply say you're wrong and let me show why. We have to say you're irredeemable and have nothing to contribute. That was the new Pharaoh's stance after the death of Joseph.

Those who succumb to the Tyrant Impulse have fallen for that age-old error of becoming evil to fight evil, but the Bible commands us to see the image of God in the most broken and hostile people (Luke 6:27-28). It directs us away from letting a good cause lead to self-righteousness, hostility, and a willingness to break other people (Luke 18:9-14; 1 John 4:19-21). According to the gospel, we must see inalienable value even in those who've devalued us. Notwithstanding Newton's Third Law, the gospel disallows the equal and opposite reaction of contempt and vengeance (Romans 12:19).

The Tyrant Impulse relies on compulsion instead of persuasion so it's obviously incompatible with democracy, but it's even more so in conflict with the gospel. Humility, respect, empathy, and intellectual honesty dismantle the Tyrant Impulse. In the public square, we must all decide whether we'll be tyrants or neighbors and advocates.

4

GETTING THE SPIRIT

ENGAGING WITH THE FRUIT OF THE SPIRIT

We don't get in the Spirit like we used to . . .
We let the devil steal our praise.

"GETTING THE SPIRIT," BY LOUISE "CANDY" DAVIS

THE SOUTHERN CHRISTIAN Leadership Conference (SCLC) followed four steps in their social action campaigns: factual determination regarding injustice, negotiation, self-purification, and direct action. The purpose of self-purification was to ensure that they were mentally and spiritually prepared to engage in a constructive manner—without bitterness or retaliation.[1] While changing systems and institutions was a major aim of the civil rights movement, there was a guiding principle that was even more important. It was the understanding that no matter how mean or nasty your opponent or the circumstances were, you could never allow them to have a negative impact on your spirit. You could win court cases and pass legislation, but in God's economy, if your spirit soured and you resorted to corruption or hate then you'd lost too much. Notwithstanding the struggle, you couldn't conform to the world's ways of handling pain and conflict. It was a test of faith.

Reverend Dr. William Augustus Jones Jr. preached this principle as he combined sound doctrine with social action in the public square. A member of Willie Faye and Mahalia's generation, he was a Baptist pastor and former president of the Progressive National Baptist Convention. He also served as first chair of the New York chapter of the SCLC, and throughout his life he was particularly focused on the struggle for human rights and economic justice. Jones was key in opening doors for jobs and racial equality in the bread and bottling industry.

Jones, a serious theologian, urged Christians to have a "nevertheless spirit." It was a spirit of aspiration, joy, and uprightness. According to him, believers with this spirit are determined to be salt and light regardless of their situation. The nevertheless spirit looks at dire circumstances and says, "nevertheless I'm stepping out on the Word of God." Dr. Jones would go on to say,

> If I listened to all the negative spirits that I've encountered in my days, had I given them a listening ear, I wouldn't have made it from here to the corner. But thanks be to God, I learned to listen with the third ear for another voice. A voice that said, you can do it with my help.[2]

Resorting to corruption or cynicism was understood as a symptom of a lack of faith. When we let those negative voices influence our public witness, we can lose hope and settle for human devices. Pessimism and fear have to be rooted out and laid to rest to achieve the social task at hand, and more importantly, to be faithful to a God who hasn't given us a spirit of fear.

FRUIT OF THE SPIRIT

The Christian public witness should be marked by aspiration and hope. The circumstances and the environment should never dictate the spirit by which we engage society. We shouldn't be oblivious to the problems we face, but we should reckon with the circumstances with an eye toward redeeming them for the better.

But we can't let the dysfunction and toxicity around us establish our standards, set the terms of engagement, or define our objectives. Our spirit doesn't come from the culture and what it considers acceptable, authentic, and praiseworthy. It comes from Jesus' teachings and the Holy Spirit, and we're bound to this narrow path even if it isn't politically expedient.

We receive the Holy Spirit through belief in Jesus as our resurrected Lord and Savior (Ephesians 1:13). True belief forces us to decenter ourselves and shift our priorities and perspectives, placing God's glory as the primary objective. The evidence of this personal transformation appears through the fruit of the Spirit. Galatians 5 says, "the fruit of the Spirit is love, joy, peace, forbearance, kindness, goodness, faithfulness, gentleness, and self-control" (Galatians 5:22-23). Unfortunately, many of these attributes are seen as weaknesses or liabilities in the culture war. We act as if the stakes are too high to be kind and patient in the public square. Ideological tribes reward pride and abrasiveness. The culture war is defined by pride, self-seeking, and what Paul referred to as "acts of the flesh," which are the opposite of the fruit of the Spirit.

Acts of the flesh include, hatred, discord, fits of rage, and selfish ambition (Galatians 5:19-21). We're warned "that those who live like this will not inherit the kingdom of God" (Galatians 5:21). Notwithstanding the apostle Paul's warning, in many instances, the Christian's public witness today is better described by "acts of the flesh" than by the fruit of the Spirit. We're merely reacting out of a sense of self-perseveration instead of applying timeless standards. The stakes are never too high to be loving and self-controlled. It's in divisive times that the fruit of the Spirit is most necessary.

FEAR AND DESPERATION

Saul's tenure as King of Israel was filled with acts of the flesh. In 1 Samuel 28, we see him descend to perhaps his lowest point. The

Bible says, "When Saul saw the Philistine army, he was afraid; terror filled his heart" (v. 5). Paranoid, terrified, and far from God, on the eve of his final battle, Saul finds himself unable to get an answer from the Lord.

It's ironic that he needs a word now because he's deliberately done everything in his power to avoid God's word up to this point. He continually ignored the prophet Samuel and he even went so far as to slaughter the priests of Nob, further silencing God. Hypocritically, Saul eventually does what he's just outlawed the rest of Israel from doing. He shamefully disguises himself and seeks a word from the witch of Endor. He's willing to invoke the dark arts to get what he wants in the moment. Predictably, Saul gets nothing but bad news, curses, and revelations of impending death. In doing things his way, Saul used evil means to achieve his objectives.

Whether we admit it, much like Saul many Christians in the public square are afraid. Conservatives are afraid of the progressive agenda, progressives are afraid of conservative agenda, and folks in the middle fear both. We've also shown a willingness to respond by utilizing the dark arts. Rather than having a nevertheless spirit, in our fear and desperation, we've embraced the spirit of the day. We seek a word from scoffers. We cheer for villains as long as they're attacking our opponents. Our politics are mean-spirited and contemptuous and we avoid God's Word when it conflicts with our cultural agenda. Christians on the Right often deemphasize the Bible's justice imperative and Christians on the Left deemphasize the Bible's sexual ethics. We consume what fits our narrative and spit out the rest.

Apparently, we believe that the situation is so dire we must be mean and dishonest to survive. We've surrendered to our circumstances. We allow cable news and social media to keep us paranoid and always enraged, not realizing that this constant state of rage makes us less thoughtful and easily manipulated. It weakens us. Few of us have literally consulted a witch, but many have sought victory through godless means. Our political opinions are often based more on party than Christian convictions.

We're not instructed to take things like economic exploitation and the sexualization of children lightly. In fact, we're negligent if we don't speak up. In Isaiah 59, God scolds Israel for not demanding justice or standing for truth. The Bible says, "The Lord looked and was displeased that there was no justice. . . . he was appalled that there was no one to intervene" (vv. 15-16). Righteous indignation is appropriate amid disorder and cruelty. That said, Ephesians 4, says, "In your anger, do not sin" (Ephesians 4:26-27). We must still display the fruit of the Spirit even when we're frustrated.

Christians can't be indifferent when faced with wickedness nor can we allow harsh realities to lead us away from a joyful and peaceful spirit. This is why Christian leaders in Willie Fay and Mahalia's generation did not encourage the people to riot even when racism caused economic deprivation, substandard housing, and police brutality.

For instance, in 1965, a six-day riot broke out in Watts, California, after the arrest of a Black man and a violent exchange between police and the crowd. Rioters overturned and burned cars and looted stores.[3] The riot resulted in an estimated forty million dollars' worth of property damage, thirty-four deaths, and four thousand arrests.[4] Dr. Martin Luther King Jr. responded to the riots by asking,

> What did Watts accomplish but the death of thirty-four Negroes and injury to thousands more? What did it profit the Negro to burn down the stores and factories in which he sought employment? The way of riots is not a way of progress, but a blind ally of death and destruction which wrecks its havoc hardest against the rioters themselves.[5]

Note, he didn't coldly condemn the rioters as if their actions weren't caused by riotous injustice in their environment. He empathized with the rioters and understood what caused them to react in such a way. The reaction wasn't worse than the cause, but it also wasn't justified by the cause. Our advocacy must reflect the fruit of the Spirit. Again, it can be tenacious, but it also must be gracious.

THE SPIRIT OF THE CAUSE

In a sermon entitled "Standing for a Cause," Dr. William Watley, the renowned AME preacher, said it this way:

> Every person—whether male or female, old or young, black or white, rich or poor, educated or uneducated, professional or common laborer—ought to stand for something. Every person ought to live for something and possess some basic principles, beliefs, and convictions that he or she is willing to die for.[6]

In the spirit of Matthew 5:16—"Let your light shine"—our Christian convictions should drive us to commit to a just and righteous cause. It's a matter of loving your neighbor, and according to 1 John 3, love is selfless and self-sacrificing (vv. 16-18). It is not just words or speech. It's active and moves us to choose compassion and truth over ourselves.

However, Christians who've been caught up in the culture war have practiced the politics of self-interest, where they seek ironclad protections for themselves while making the needs of others an afterthought. Conversely, the Bible says, "In humility value others over yourselves, not looking to your own interests but each of you to the interests of the others" (Philippians 2:3-4). This is particularly true for how we treat our brothers and sisters in Christ, but it's also true for how we should treat our neighbors.

Our causes don't have to disregard our own interest, but they should be evidence of the self-sacrificial love we have for others. For instance, when we advocate for religious liberty, it shouldn't be just for ourselves, but also for our Muslim and Hindu neighbors. This isn't because we affirm their beliefs. In fact we should be willing to profess our disagreement in love, but we also protect those we disagree with.

Dr. Watley also noted that standing for something is risky and "we need to be very sure that the cause that we're sacrificing for is worth . . . the price we are paying."[7] Christians must evaluate the objectives of the movement before committing themselves to it or espousing it. A good cause and good intentions are insufficient because they don't guarantee righteous means. It's a mistake to judge a movement solely by its publicly professed cause and stated objectives. The spirit of the movement must also be examined. Is the cause seeking redemption or vengeance? Are their opponents treated with respect or contempt? As Christians, we must test the spirits. The Bible says we'll recognize false teaching by its fruit—"A good tree cannot bear bad fruit, and a bad tree cannot bear good fruit" (Matthew 7:15-18).

Furthermore, the spirit of a movement can descend morally. It might start off fruitful but later succumb to darker tactics. For instance, Robert Moses, the infamous New York urban planner, started off as a well-meaning, Oxford-educated reformer fighting against corruption, but because of the corruption in the city, he found it difficult to get good things done.[8] Eventually, he got frustrated and decided to accomplish his objectives through deception and oppressive power. He became a greedy powerbroker who served himself and his cronies. He created an environment that treated poor people like rats—trapping them in deleterious slums and traumatizing generations of image bearers.

In our brokenness, all of us are at risk of experiencing this kind of transition. Consequently, we must continually examine our attitudes, motives, and character. Engaging with the right spirit keeps things in perspective. It keeps us humble and aware of our tendency to become self-interested. It reminds us that we are not perfectly righteous, and our opposition is not completely evil. The goal is to glorify God, not to receive some sort of salvation through our social action.

The issue with the culture war isn't that the cause is always wrong, but it's often pursued in the wrong spirit, and, therefore, becomes corrupted. This is likely why when some Americans hear the term *family values* they think of a "political ploy, a way to win votes, or a phony issue."[9] Compassionately working to preserve a biblical definition of family and sexual morality is good, but when that objective is advanced without the fruit of the Spirit, the entire movement is compromised. Instead of displaying a patient and gentle public witness, the spirit of the Moral Majority was hostile, holier-than-thou, and full of condemnation.

This is all too clear in how Moral Majority leader, Jerry Falwell spoke about feminists:

> I listen to feminists and all these radical gals—most of them are failures. They've blown it. Some of them have been married, but they married some Casper Milquetoast who asked permission to go to the bathroom. These women just need a man in the house. That's all they need. Most of the feminists need a man to tell them what time of day it is and to lead them home. And they blew it and they're mad at all men.[10]

That statement is completely void of the fruit of the Spirit. It better reflects the hatred and discord associated with acts of the flesh. It turns all women who identify as feminists into caricatures. Doing so is not only unloving but also untruthful. Some aspects of feminism should be challenged, but in a more compassionate and respectful manner.

One of the most highly esteemed Black Baptist preachers, Dr. C. A. W. Clark, warned us about what happens when the Holy Spirit departs:

> Keep the Holy Spirit with you. For when the Holy Spirit departs, you have sound but not substance. When the Holy Spirit departs, the place of meeting becomes just a meeting place. When the Holy Spirit departs, you have movement and activity, but not progress. Keep the Holy Spirit with you in your life and in your living.[11]

A Christian movement without love, peace, kindness, and self-control is just as dangerous as a toxic secular movement.

Social justice movements aren't immune to acts of the flesh either. Pastor Jim Jones, founder of the People's Temple, appeared to be completely committed to desegregation, class equality, and several other social justice causes. He often preached about tolerance and liberation. He professed the social gospel and said socialism was good because it "brought perfect justice, freedom and equality."[12] He also fiercely attacked White evangelical churches that weren't fighting against America's racist system.

For some social-justice-oriented Christians, that's all they need to hear to believe the leader and movement are righteous. It wasn't all talk: "Jones desegregated movie theaters, restaurants, the telephone company, hospitals, and the [Indianapolis] police department."[13] His church also owned and operated homes for the elderly and mentally ill. But the spirit of his movement was wicked, marred by selfish ambition, lies, and sexual abuse. He'd eventually persuade or force over 900 people to commit what he called "revolutionary suicide."[14]

Nothing about the words *social* or *justice* have the power to save us. No magic words or topic make an initiative righteous. It's the spirit and substance of the effort that are important, and those things must reflect the fruit of the Spirit. This is the problem with Jim Jones' iteration of the social gospel—it makes our work more important than our faith in and obedience to God and his Word. If your social engagement causes you to reject the authority of

Scripture, it's counterproductive and you're discipling backwards. Acts of the flesh make us feel like saviors, but the fruit of the Spirit glorifies God and highlights that he's the savior. Dr. Watley put it this way:

> We must never forget that none of these movements can in and of themselves save our souls. That's why I think of that which is basic, first, and ultimate to my life, I've decided to make Jesus my choice. It is only as one seeks first the kingdom of God and its righteousness that one is truly liberated to work in history and in one's existential situation for the justice that is intrinsic to Christ's vision of a fully consummated kingdom.[15]

SCOFFERS AND BITTERNESS

The Bible has a lot to say about scoffers. Psalm 1 says, "Blessed is the man who walks not in the counsel of the wicked, nor stands in the way of sinners, nor sits in the seat of scoffers" (v. 1 ESV). Proverbs rebukes the scoffer—"condemnation is ready for scoffers" (19:29 ESV). A scoffer is one who mocks and derides others. They're scornful, prideful, and arrogant. They show utter contempt for others. This is a group that clearly doesn't operate under the right spirit as they dishonor others and use their words to bring others low and exalt themselves. Their words and outlook are bitter.

Today, we often praise the most cynical voices, those who are witty with their insults and most cutting with their disparagement of others. In 2024, many of us cheered when congresswomen Marjorie Taylor Greene and Jasmine Crockett disparaged each other's appearances in a committee hearing.[16] What does it say about us that we find joy in that? When someone whose politics we dislike goes to jail or is exposed for corruption, we celebrate as if that were our communion. We rejoice in the humiliation of our opponents and elected officials, and candidates are always trying to supply us with those moments. Congressional hearings are wasted by elected officials play acting so they can get a viral clip.

But Proverbs condemns the activity of the scoffer and the scornful as an abomination to the people (Proverbs 24:9), and sadly, the people who claim to be representing the poor, the weak, and the unborn do a disservice to those groups because their words are scornful, contemptuous, or unnecessarily extreme. Bad behaving advocates do the people they claim to represent a disservice. Discipline isn't a vice and measured words are a sign of complacency.

Proverbs 16:21 says, "The wise of heart is called discerning" (ESV), and gracious words increase persuasiveness. It is wise to be gracious and judicious in how we address others if our intention is truly to persuade them to do right. No one is convinced to have a change of heart by someone who is belligerent and loveless in their social action. The heart of the wise makes his speech judicious and adds persuasiveness to his lips. If we want to be an asset to our cause, we don't have to be less tenacious, but we do need to be more gracious. No one is persuaded by insults. If we're in the Spirit, our public witness and social action should be worship. It should be uplifting and full of joy.

DECENCY, DIGNITY, AND RESILIENCE

Born in 1879, Nannie Helen Burroughs grew up in poverty, but her formerly enslaved mother made sure she was educated and imbued with a sense of dignity. She'd become an educator, writer, and speaker who'd challenge sexism in her denomination—National Baptist Convention—and found the National Training School for Women and Girls and the National Association of Wage Earners.[17]

Scholar Kelisha Graves explains, "Christian theology served as the dominant infrastructure thought which [Burroughs] articulated every other major idea in her life."[18] A suffragist and civil rights advocate, she understood that it wasn't enough to just be free; we also need to have a spirit of virtue and honor. No situation justified indecency. She refused to coddle or pander to her community. She loved them with her daily work, resources, and by her insistence on living by a dignified standard. She spoke "the truth in love" (Ephesians 4:15).

Burroughs sternly instructed the Black community to commit to the "development of character traits" and "become eager and determined to improve mentally, morally and spiritually, and to meet the basic requirements of good citizenship." She rebuked White America for "penalizing Negroes for not being white . . . Color isn't character."[19] She also rebuked the Black community for "undermin[ing] [its] spiritual and moral vitality" by focusing on material matters "at the expense of higher virtues."[20]

She didn't pull any punches, but her intent was always upliftment rather than belittlement. Her words show us how serious she was about honor in the face of physical and moral threats:

> The honor of black womanhood is at stake, and let those who will, cower before the crisis, but let us here, in this place put ourselves on record as protectors and defenders of Christian womanhood.[21]

In accordance with the tradition, Burroughs showed that injustice didn't have to lead the oppressed to a spirit of indecency. She was determined to hold her community to a higher standard because she wanted them to flourish. She was a defender of Black dignity and a cultivator of Black self-regard and betterment.

Again, not all responses to injustice are constructive, just, or justifiable. Some movements are so distorted they can't tell the difference between virtues and vices, or they've broadened the definition of some vices to include what are really virtues. For example, the culture has rightly rejected the pursuit of respectability or respectability politics. *Respectability* is trying to make one's identity group look more proper in the eyes of majority culture based on its cultural norms and standards. *Respectability politics* expects to benefit from this assimilation. The pushback against this approach was wise because respectability establishes parts of White culture as the standard, leaving everyone else to behave, dress, and communicate in accordance with their norms to gain acceptance and be worthy of respect.

The truth is we're already worthy of a measure of respect due to human dignity, and no one race or class's culture should dictate the standard of what is considered appropriate in a pluralistic society. For too long, the cultures of Black and Brown people have been deemed lesser based on the arbitrary preferences and criteria of majority culture. For instance, one shouldn't have to properly speak the King's English or a predominately White dialect to be heard and respected in the public square.

However, the concept of respectability has become so broad that it's started to crowd out certain virtues. We've placed traits under the umbrella of respectability that are basic standards of courtesy and uprightness. The establishment of standards, in general, isn't necessarily the promotion of respectability politics. Some have taken the rejection of respectability to mean behaving, dressing, and communicating in any way we feel should never be critiqued but always celebrated. However, we can't do away with common decency. This also comes with a cultural relativism that says if a behavior is native to a certain culture, critiquing it is bigoted. It's gone so far that being purposefully indecent and irreverent has become a sign of authenticity. Violating reasonable standards of decorum is commended. It's a badge of honor to intentionally act in a way that offends majority culture.

As Christians, we must strive to be upright, decent, and dignified without becoming self-righteous or weighing down others with heavy burdens (Titus 2:2; 1 Timothy 3:11; Matthew 23:4). We should seek to be dignified without being prideful or vain. We don't need purity culture, but we should have standards that discourage sexual immorality and debauchery (Galatians 5:19). We have to be careful where we draw those lines, but surely there's a line that needs to be drawn for the sake of ordered and healthy community.

A desire to be completely untethered in how we behave, dress, and communicate is a sign of a toxic form of individualism and selfishness. If we have a spirit that loves and honors others, then it can't be all about our individual expression. For instance, not cussing in front of elders or children isn't about external approval, it's about honoring our elders and practicing self-control for the sake of our children's' development. This doesn't mean we ignore the voice of those who violate that standard, but correcting them in love isn't respectability politics. Parents who take their children to a sports game shouldn't have to expose them to scantily clad women twerking in the row next to them. We should all cringe when we see men catcalling women in front of their children.

We disrespect ourselves when we confuse dignity with respectability. Respectability is superficial, but dignity is about the value God placed inside of us. Respectability is proving your worthiness to others. Dignity is a sense of self-worth. It's indicative of the spirit we have inside of us working on the outside of us. We're to carry ourselves with decency and integrity not because we're seeking validation from majority culture, but because we're innately valuable and serve a God who's upright. This doesn't mean we have to wear suits and dress shoes every day. It's not about a specific way of dressing. It's about exuding self-worth and respecting others.

I FEEL LIKE GOING ON—RESILIENCE

Thirty-four mass lynchings are documented during the Reconstruction Era, when Black preachers like Congressman Richard H.

Cain and Senator Hiram R. Revels stepped into office. In two Louisiana parishes alone over two hundred Black people were killed leading up to an election.[22] In 1921, Black Wall Street in Greenwood, Oklahoma, was burned to the ground due to nothing more than covetousness from Whites.[23] In the early 1960s, the bombing of Black homes and churches were so frequent in the city of Birmingham, Alabama, that it earned the name "Bombingham."[24] This includes the bombing of the 16th Street Baptist Church, where four young girls were killed.

Each of those occurrences was meant to send a message to the Black: *No matter what you do, you will not prosper. If you dare to exercise the right to vote, we'll lynch you. If you build an economic marvel, we'll burn it down with impunity. If you raise up a leader, we'll kill him. If you find solace in the sanctuary, we'll bomb that too. You have no history and you have no future outside of a thorough bleaching of culture and soul. Give up!*

The attacks on churches were especially heinous. Of those instances, civil rights activist Ozell Sutton said,

> The attack on African American churches is more than just an act of terrorism against a place of worship . . . It is an attack on the very soul of the African American community. It is the source of their sense of human, their sense of self-worth, their struggle for dignity and equality.[25]

This terrorism was meant to overcome the spirit of the Black community and break it down completely, but the story of the Black Church is one of courage and resilience. Hypersensitivity wasn't an option. When Mahalia Jackson's CBS show was canceled because Southern audiences didn't want a Black woman on national television, she still had the fortitude to encourage Dr. Martin Luther King Jr. to keep fighting righteously.[26] They were afflicted but refused to wallow in self-pity.

Jesus cared deeply about the afflicted. He treated the blind, the paralyzed, lepers, and those suffering from other maladies with great sympathy, caring for them and healing them (Matthew 4:24). Accordingly, it's good that society and the church are de-stigmatizing issues like mental illness. In the past, too many people suffered in silence, afraid to be shamed for seeking professional help. In many cases, this is an example of where the church had to learn from people outside the church. Let us be humbled and thankful in acknowledging that. We're still learning to encourage people to ask for therapy when needed. We should expand those efforts.

Unfortunately, in our brokenness, humanity tends to find a fix and push it into excess. We have a habit of melting down useful tools and fashioning them into idols. We see a good thing like being open about our struggles and pervert it into seeking attention and gaining status for our struggles.

San Francisco social worker and mental health therapist Pamela Garfield-Jaegar fears we've gone from de-stigmatizing mental illness to celebrating it. She's dedicated her life to suicide prevention and mental health, and now believes it's become fashionable to have mental illness.

> Today, mental health issues are celebrated. People broadcast their diagnosis on their social media pages. Mental illness is glorified on TV and in film. Celebrities get more attention when they speak publicly about their mental health issues. As a result, people often self-diagnose, just to feel a part of something . . . The word "affirm" is used WAY too often nowadays. In addition, kids are learning to play up their mental health issues because they learn they will get excused from important life challenges unchecked.[27]

These days, people throw around words like *trauma, triggered,* and *PTSD* liberally. These conditions and terms should be taken seriously, which is why using them outside of the clinical meaning causes a problem. It causes lesser offenses and wounds to be perceived as more impactful than they have to be. If we tell people words are violence and classic books like *Huck Finn* and *Things Fall Apart* are triggering, then we lower their sense of resilience.[28]

Thankfully, most people can withstand an insult, racial epithet, or the description of a traumatic historical event without being traumatized themselves. But our hypersensitivity is unduly lowering our pain threshold to the point where we're less likely to have the will to fight through the inevitable battles of life.[29] We'll run from things we have the ability to fight through. The stress of an upcoming examination becomes a breakdown when that doesn't have to be the case. An insult becomes catastrophic when it could build character. In sum, we're weakening ourselves by overstating the damage done by painful yet bearable encounters.

In the face of segregation, disenfranchisement, and lynch mobs, Willie Fay and Mahalia's generation is known for their resilience. The Bible urged them to "be strong and courageous," and they followed those orders as a matter of faith (Joshua 1:9). One of the student leaders of the civil rights struggle in Albany was arrested and mistreated in jail. After she was released, she received word from Albany State, where she was attending college, that she had been suspended indefinitely as a result of the arrest. As she described her experience, she said,

> I felt it was necessary to show the people that human dignity must be obtained even if through suffering or maltreatment. . . . I'd do it again anytime. . . . After spending those two nights in jail for a worthy cause, I feel that I have gained a feeling of decency and self-respect, a feeling of cleanliness that even the dirtiest walls of Albany's jail nor the actions of my institution take away from me.[30]

They also knew love consoles us and challenges us as a means of equipping us (Psalm 23:4; Luke 9:1-27). They didn't hide the harsh reality of racism from us, nor were we enabled to use it as an excuse for our shortcomings.

In the 1950s, Clay Evans launched and grew Fellowship Baptist in Chicago. Evans was a pioneer in gospel music and a respected preacher and community leader. He had a good working relationship with Mayor Richard Daley and the leadership of the city. In the 1960s, "the Ship" had grown so much that the church needed to expand, and Evans ran a successful capital campaign to raise the initial funds for the expansion and secured a loan for the rest. But in 1965, as the building project was underway, Evans endorsed the campaign of Martin Luther King Jr. to improve housing conditions for African Americans in Chicago, who were subjected to redlining and other forms of housing discrimination.

He immediately found himself estranged from Daley, and he was told in no uncertain terms that if did not turn on King, the loan would be rescinded. Evans refused, and immediately all permits were withdrawn and the loan was canceled. For seven years, Evans and his congregation worshiped in the shadow of the steel skeleton of the new building. Each week he would remind his people that "even in these times of tribulation, the Lord is with us. He has something he wants us to learn." He immersed his people in the narrative of Scripture, urging them to see themselves as the Israelites wandering in the desert: "These days are to us what the wilderness was to the children of Israel . . . They will bring us closer to the Lord. We can do for ourselves what we thought only other folk could do for us."[31]

Many years after the completion of the building project, Evans's sister Lou Della, who was choir leader at the Ship for many years, reflected on this season:

> We had to leave the building for seven years. But was using that in another way for us. "I need to build you spiritually. I

> need to make you stronger. You got some growing to do." But we know that it was God that took us through it and then gave us the say so: "Go ahead. I'm going to build it now. I have built you. I need to build you before I build the building." So that's what he did. He built us before he built the building.[32]

The travail that Evans and Fellowship went through for these seven years shows what resilience can accomplish. The well-intentioned effort to insulate people from suffering actually robs them of the capacity to respond to difficult situations creatively and innovatively.

Coddling is a distorted conception of love because it tries in vain to shield us from reality and truth. Coddling is quite possibly connected to the rise in depression among young people, which means our distorted sense of compassion could be creating mental health issues rather than solving them.[33]

We should be sensitive to the suffering of others while instilling a spirit of resilience. We must protect those around us without resorting to *safetyism*—the idea that safety is a sacred "value."[34] This leads to an unwillingness to make the trade-offs necessary for "practical and moral concerns."[35] For example, if you never allow your child to play outside with others, they may not get sick or hurt (they'll be safe), but they also won't build antibodies, nor will they be socialized. This is counterproductive in the long term because they won't develop the resistance and skills necessary to protect themselves in the future. Accordingly, the answer is neither recklessness nor safetyism. We should protect our children without going to the extreme of coddling. That dynamic also relates to how we should think about culture more broadly.

If we're to love like Jesus loved, then we'll care for people without hiding the truth or celebrating affliction. Jesus loved deeply, but he didn't coddle. He told the disabled man at the Pool of Bethesda to get up and walk and to "sin no more" (John 5:14 ESV). When discussing the prostitute who anointed his feet, Jesus said, "Her many sins have been forgiven" (Luke 7:47). In both cases, Jesus acted in love, but he did so without hiding the truth. He pitied them, but he respected their dignity enough to inform them about the reality of their situations.

For Willie Fay and Mahalia's generation, resilience was a matter of survival. Despite violence and setbacks, they refused to quit pursuing justice and a more perfect union. Marvin Winans's song, "I Feel Like Going On" captures their resolve:

> I feel like going on going on, even though trials,
> They may come on every hand I feel,
> I feel like going, I feel like going on.[36]

Through scientific advances, our understanding of mental illness has grown past what was available to Willie Fay and Mahalia's generation. The church must have the intellectual humility to admit that. We must also continue to construct a space for therapy and mental health to grow into the resilience ethic they taught America. Never should we downplay the pain of the afflicted and tell them to "just be strong." Most of us aren't qualified to determine when someone has mental illness, but in general, we can destigmatize mental illness while celebrating resilience. We can protect without being over-protective.

5

JESUS, YOU'RE THE CENTER

CENTERING THE FAITH IN OUR CULTURAL AND POLITICAL ENGAGEMENT

IN 1933, AME BISHOP REVERDY C. RANSOM convened Black Church denominational leaders to discuss creating an organization to initiate united action and be an authoritative voice on "social, economic, industrial, and political questions."[1] The coalition he envisioned would be named the Fraternal Council of Negro Churches. It was one of the first national Black Church organizations of its kind and laid groundwork for cross-denominationalism in social action. It was an explicitly nonpartisan organization that believed that the public square securing justice was the "appropriate measure of faithfulness not only in the white church, but of the Black Church as well."[2]

The group's ethic clearly reflected the "love of neighbor" and "love of enemy" biblical mandates. Even while facing racial terrorism, the Council's "Address to the Country" made it clear that they were about cooperation not antagonism:

> We would not . . . have it understood that by urging organization along racial lines we are urging antagonism to the white people of our country. Far be it from that. We are offering the only method of cooperating with white people. The Negroes cannot hope to cooperate individually, but only collectively.[3]

The Pittsburgh Courier called it "mobilized Christian theology in action."[4] The Council was a religious organization applying their faith in helping the underprivileged and oppressed. At the center of the mission were the teachings of Christ, which also served as the framework for engagement. Historian Mary Sawyer explained that their social action was "preceded by theological reflection, and theological reflection by the experienced authenticity of the faith."[5]

Sawyer further stated that many Black religious leaders and organizations like the Council refused to endorse particular ideologies or identify with a political label, "invoking instead a transcendent, biblically grounded ethic of justice."[6] For them, ideologies and political movements were often compromised by bias and self-interest. They weren't interested in being in the middle of the partisan squabbles and ideological rivalries of the time. They were pursuing justice and equality, not seeking to bolster either party or prove some conservative or progressive point.

At the same time, there was also a practical value in having conversations and relationships with all sides in power. The civil rights movement engaged presidents Richard Nixon and John F. Kennedy when trying to pass civil rights legislation.[7] Furthermore, when Congressman J. C. Watts was the only Black Republican in Congress and was considering leaving, he received a letter from civil rights legend Rosa Parks imploring him to stay for the sake of representation: "If you can, please remain as a pioneer on the Republicans' side until others come to assist you. I am glad I stayed in my seat."[8] Like the Council, faith should be the center of our public witness, but if we're not careful, partisanship and antagonism will replace it.

CHOOSE A SIDE!

Colossians 2:8 says, "See to it that no one takes you captive through hollow and deceptive philosophy, which depends on human tradition and the elemental spiritual forces of this world rather than on Christ." Partisan agendas and ideology too often capture our public witness in a way the Bible forbids. We're constantly pressured to display unconditional alignment with the ideological Left or Right. If we don't, our peers will ridicule us for naiveté or cancel us for untrustworthiness. Moreover, to agree or work with the other side on anything is to be completely tainted. You'll be called a Marxist by Conservatives or a bigot by Progressives for disagreeing with any element of their stances. Like a gang, you must choose a side and like a cult, you can't question the leadership or agenda.

These groups can be ungodly, but they frown on lukewarmness as if they had God's authority and righteousness. Even if their position is illogical or unreasonably extreme, you're expected to be on fire for it or face the consequences—you're either totally with them or against them.

The culture war teaches us that culture and politics are a zero-sum, winner-take-all battle between the Left and the Right. Accordingly, on every issue, your side is either winning or losing ground. A critique of one side is often interpreted as an endorsement of other, but that's not always the case. One might critique Republicans and still feel Democrats are too extreme or insufficient on the same issue, and vice versa.

To be clear, I agree that Christians who are neutral on issues of justice and morality are wrong. There is nothing inherently righteous about a moderate or middle-ground position. If moderation is a means of conflict avoidance or taking the path of least resistance, then it too is sinful. We can't be fence-sitters when it comes to addressing injustice and immorality.

However, neither side has a perfect record on justice or moral order (which will be detailed in later chapters). They may not be equivalent on any given issue, but they both have significant flaws that can blind and contaminate our engagement. It's no mystery why a thoughtful Christian might find themselves somewhere in the middle of the wide divide between a group who ignores the physiological distinctions between the sexes and a group who treats America's history of sexism and racism as a myth. But the point isn't to find the middle position, it's to locate and stand for what's right.

Frederick Douglass, the Christian abolitionist and former slave famously said, "I would unite with anybody to do right and with nobody to do wrong." That shrewd quote completely dismantles the rationale behind choosing a side in the culture war. Our side can be right about ninety-nine things, but as a Christians, we can't justify or work with them on the one thing they get wrong. We also can't disagree or discredit our opponents on the one thing they get right.

Those trying to force us to choose between the ideological Left and Right have confused choosing a side with choosing the right position. As discussed in chapter 3, this is not simply a choice of good versus evil. Therefore, a Christian can reject the two primary ideological tribes while taking firm positions on important issues and working toward solutions, or they can generally support one side, but they can't uncritically support them on every issue and be faithful. Since the Council's stance didn't center a party or ideological tribe, they were able to apply Christian principles and logic more faithfully to each issue.

When it came to justice, the Black Church social action tradition didn't allow partisan or ideological allegiances to compromise the ultimate goal. The Chicago Baptist pastor Donald Parson was described as "among the most socially active pastors of his generation."[9] He pioneered and promoted what he called "ministry to the total man," similar to what René Padilla called "integral mission."[10] He was an early supporter of Jesse Jackson Sr. and the work of Operation Breadbasket and the P.U.S.H. Coalition in Chicago. But when his congregation, Mount Calvary Church, sought to improve education for African Americans in the city by opening a church-based K-8 school, he did not hesitate to learn best practices from White conservatives.

Parson observed that Jerry Falwell Sr. and Jack Hyles had both developed successful schools attached to their congregations and attended one of their conferences on Christian education. Parson went so far as to develop a relationship with Jack Hyle, who pastored in Hammond, Indiana, and their friendship resulted in a gradual change in Hyles who "started to make people available to help teach our deaf ministry and to help get our bus ministry started."[11]

Parson did not cease to emphasize the biblical imperative to demolish segregationist policies and attitudes, nor did he pursue relationship with Hyles naively or uncritically. He was simply humble enough to understand that in this one arena the Holy Spirit was urging collaboration and that refusing to learn from these believers would impoverish his church's efforts for educational excellence in their community.

Dr. Martin Luther King was staying true to this tradition when he criticized conservatives, liberals, and moderates for their views on race and justice. In his "Letter from a Birmingham Jail," he admonished conservatives who were upset about the protests but didn't seem to show the same concern for "the conditions that brought the demonstrations into being." He also cited them for telling the protesters to follow the law while they ignored the US Supreme Court's *Brown v. Board* decision.[12]

In the same letter, he rebuked moderates for being more devoted to order than justice and "paternalistically feel[ing] he can set the timetable for another man's freedom."[13] He also called out northern liberals for their polite racism:

> As the nation, Negro and white, trembled with outrage at police brutality in the South, police misconduct in the

> North was rationalized, tolerated, and usually denied. Leaders in Northern and Western states welcomed me to their cities, and showered praise on the heroism of Southern Negroes. Yet when the issues were joined concerning local conditions, only the language was polite; the rejection was firm and unequivocal.[14]

Furthermore, if Christians are always "just choosing a side," then we're never leading. Our political sect of choice is leading us and we're simply cosigning their agenda. Willie Faye and Mahalia's generation knew it was time to lead because neither the Right, the Left, nor the middle had the answers. How can Christians be the conscience of the nation like the civil rights movement if we're not willing to lead? Following the world when justice and truth are on the line is intellectually lazy and unfaithful.

Not unconditionally choosing a side doesn't mean we're indecisive, unaware, or inactive. It can simply mean that we see the nuance in issues and the flaws on the Left and Right. As convicted and thoughtful Christians, we should be able to support Republicans if they get parental rights correct while rejecting their position on healthcare. Similarly, we can support Democrats if they get voter rights correct while rejecting their abortion policy.

To settle for simply choosing a side is to wrongly assume one side of the culture war always gets it right or right enough. However, there are often more than two possible solutions to our problems. Therefore, both sides could be wrong on a given issue and they can also be wrong when they agree or act in unison. We can see this in the student loans crisis and the 2008 economic crisis. Democratic and Republican leaders supported policies that led to these crises. Accordingly, Christians who settled for just choosing a side got it wrong and millions of Americans are still suffering because of it. A more prophetic witness might've disagreed with both and offered a more thoughtful alternative.

The Bible never obligates us to choose a political or cultural sect, but it does obligate us to "do justice" and "be holy" (Micah 6:8; 1 Peter 1:15-16). The gospel disallows any allegiance that might get in the way of doing God's will (Matthew 18:9). Glorifying God by being righteous and just in the public square should be our focus over any side. Furthermore, Jesus didn't just choose a side. He didn't become a Sadducee because the Pharisees were judgmental, and he didn't become a Pharisee because of the Sadducee's unbelief. Jesus never made it about pledging support to one flawed group over another. Without qualification, he told us to take care of the poor, love our neighbor, and love our enemy (Mark 10:21-22; 12:30-31; Matthew 5:43-44). He corrected the religiously conservative Pharisees, the elite Sadducees, and the worldly Herodians (Matthew 23:5-7; Mark 12:13-17). He stood on principles and honestly critiqued insiders and outsiders impartially.

THE GOSPEL OVER PARTISANSHIP AND IDEOLOGY

When addressing the Democratic Party's stances on family and sexual ethics, Bishop G. E. Patterson, the former presiding leader of the Church of God in Christ, told his congregation that Christians "have to be careful not to let your political ties be stronger than your religious convictions."[15] Since neither party nor ideology is a pure application of the gospel, the agenda of both sides will come into conflict with Christian principles. When that tension arises, Christians must choose Christian principles over partisanship and ideological conclusions. Ultimately, our duty in the sociopolitical arena isn't to be the best Democrat or Republican we can be, but to glorify God by representing his justice and truth faithfully.

The truth is many Christians have trouble understanding politics and their own public witness outside of the culture war framework. Every decision with cultural or political implications seems like a choice between conservatism and progressivism, and in many cases, rather than considering the issues through the lens of biblical principles, we summarily follow one side or the other. But those culture war categories can limit us. We end up trying to define and evaluate our civic activity by measures and models that can't capture the full brilliance of a gospel-centered witness. Like when applying a foreign standard of beauty to our physical features, we'll never see ourselves as God intended, nor will we confidently exist in our calling on culture war terms. A Christian limited to the boundaries of the ideological Left and Right has a distorted and fragmented witness.

The idea that we must be entirely progressive or conservative on every issue is a ploy to control our cultural and political opinions. If cultural influencers can get us to base our opinions on ideological identity rather than critical analysis and convictions, then they control our public witness. Once we start proudly wearing the label, critical thinking is no longer necessary. They'll do all the thinking for us and we'll simply rubber stamp their conclusions. But the church must be convicted and thoughtful enough to have prophetic independence.

Focusing on choosing the right position instead of choosing a side helps us avoid ideological capture. It allows us to center Christian principles and find common cause with others without having to pledge full allegiance or overlook wrongdoing. We can participate in party politics while having the independence to challenge and correct behavior and policy in conflict with truth and compassion.

IDEOLOGICAL TRIBALISM

When discussing works of the flesh, Paul mentions what the English Standard Version refers to as "rivalries" (Galatians 5:20). These are quarrels caused by self-seeking. They divert our eyes from what's good and true, shifting our focus toward spiting those who stand in the way of us gaining worldly advantage. Preoccupied with antagonism and winning the argument, we devalue doing what's right. The fight becomes more important than the solution.[16] Tribal rivalries center on our contempt for one another and make our disputes more about spite than the merits of the argument.

Tribalism is loyalty to a social group, "especially when combined with strong negative feelings for people outside the group."[17] Writer Thomas Freidman referred to tribalism as a virus infesting our democracy by making it difficult for diverse groups to work together.[18] Tribalism can cause us to obsess over and antagonize opponents and uncritically support our side when they're wrong. Loyalty to our ideological tribe can cause us to place the tribe's interests, narratives, and rivalries above Christian principles. It becomes the center of our engagement, replacing the love and truth of Christ.

How have we allowed our rivalries to become the center of our public witness? The answer is we've become obsessed with proving our political opponents are completely evil, responsible for all societal wrongs, and must be humiliated. We've become opposition centered. Through cable news, talk radio, and social media, we've come to believe our opponents are virtually incapable of sincerity and good works. Their every word and action are meant to either harm, deceive, or control us. They're not just occasionally wrong—they're always wrong, which means what's right is found on the opposite side of their every belief and opinion. This is what I call opposition-centered engagement—forming our beliefs and selecting our positions based on a desire to create as much distance as possible between us and our opponents. Ironically, this places the people we disdain most at the center of our decision-making process.[19]

We've confused fighting those who we think are wrong with doing what's right. Wrongdoers should be opposed, but we should never become evil to fight evil. Like Maximilien Robespierre massacring corrupt aristocrats during the French Revolution, we can become the villain while fighting villains. While some of us choose a side and become tribal due to peer pressure or a failure to think critically, others do it simply because they hate the other side. Political scientists Alan Abramowitz and Steven Webster labeled this phenomenon "negative partisanship."[20] They found, "A growing number of Americans have been voting against the opposing party rather than for their own party."[21] Our political identities are increasingly aligned with social, cultural, and political divisions in American society.[22] We're basing identity in the public square on who we dislike instead of the character and will of God.

Our opposition-centered posture also controls our opinions. For instance, we'll reject a policy we would've otherwise supported if the policy is sponsored by a leader on the other side. For example, before Obamacare was Obamacare, Senator Mitt Romney proposed a healthcare plan that was very similar to it.[23] Romney himself said, "Without Romneycare, I don't think we would have Obamacare."[24] Conservatives who were open to Romneycare outright opposed Obamacare. Instead of focusing on principles and solutions, our attitudes, behavior, and policy are suffering because we've centered our opponents in our public witness.

Furthermore, much of our communication is meant to motivate our side through rage, fear, and contempt rather than persuade the other side. Some influencers appear to spend most of their time searching high and low for examples of other groups' worst behavior—White women or "Karens" caught on video screaming false accusations, or Black men robbing old ladies. These displays serve to inflame the tensions by maintaining stereotypes and keeping us enraged, and the advent of social media has caused us to lose our sense of proximity and proportion. Consequently, all these things seem like they're happening next door and every hour, even if the video is an isolated incident from across the country years ago.

The Bible says, "Everyone should be quick to listen, slow to speak and slow to become angry, because human anger does not produce the righteousness that God desires" (James 1:19-20). Unfortunately, we're slow to listen, quick to speak, and constantly infuriated by our opposition. While Christians can be righteously indignant about injustice and immorality, a Christian shouldn't stay in a state of rage. Among other things, when we're enraged, we're easily manipulated. There's less room for a sound critique so we're less thoughtful, less constructive, and less compassionate. Again, the dynamic is aggravated by social media. Based on social media algorithms, "posts that trigger emotions—especially anger at out-groups—are the most likely to be shared."[25]

Our spiteful rivalries distort our values and lure us into intellectual dishonesty. When we've centered our contempt for opponents, we're slower to speak truths that conflict with our side's conclusions because we don't want our opponents to win or get any credit. We'll deny when the other side is right and find rationalizations for supporting our side when they're wrong.

Even when the stakes were the highest, Frederick Douglass was willing to admit when his side was wrong. He even critiqued other abolitionists. His position was clear—he wanted slavery abolished. But he wasn't so beholden to an abolitionist organization's point of view that he was unwilling to disagree with them. He publicly disagreed with William Lloyd Garrison and the American Anti-Slavery Society about dissolving the union and opposing the US Constitution.[26] Taking a position didn't mean uncritically going along with all assertions of the group you agree with most. As a former slave, he had the moral imagination and courage to disagree with other abolitionists when they were wrong. He didn't mute himself in fear that it'd be interpreted as a win for the pro-slavery side. He said what he believed was right. That takes an incredible amount of integrity and faith and that's what cross-bearing in the public square demands.

The Bible also tells us doing right sometimes involves standing against the crowd and those with whom we share an identity and interests. Jesus made zealots and tax collectors abandon their associations to follow him (Luke 5:27-28). Paul had to stand against his former circle once he saw the light and had to testify to the truth (Acts 23). Our public witness must clearly stake out the right positions and work toward the solutions that further our calling.

EMPTY DEFIANCE AND MORALITY BY COMPARISON

When we've made our opponents symbols for all that is wrong and evil in society, we begin to form our identities around being their opposite. For example, many social justice–oriented Christians not only dislike the racism and sexism in White evangelicalism, but we've also resolved to disagree with them on all other issues too. If they legitimately point out the sexualization of children by popular culture, we'll deny it exists or go so far as to embrace it. We'll literally ignore the corruption of children to avoid admitting the other side is right. At that point, we're no longer upholding truth or serving God.

These rivalries cause us to find a false virtue in taking the opposite position. Once we've chosen a side, to be caught agreeing with the other side on anything is ignorant, treasonous, or immoral. This is used to manipulate us. A conservative leader can turn his side against a good policy just by saying progressives support it without actually making a cogent argument himself, and when someone makes a good argument against a progressive position, they can just say "that's a conservative talking point" and their side will dismiss it.

In our contempt, we not only hate our opponent's vices, but we also begin to hate their virtues. This is the warping effect of opposition-centered engagement. The good they do can't be acknowledged because it might compromise our narrative or give them a win. We only acknowledge their excesses. Many on the Right can't appreciate the work the Left has done for women's rights. They only acknowledge the influence of extreme forms of feminism. The Left can't appreciate the culture in some White evangelical circles of adopting children from all over the world. This should be seen as a sign of compassion, but the Left will find a way to make it yet another sign of an impulse to dominate.

We don't just want to take the opposite position; we want to offend the other side and parade our contempt for them in the public square. For instance, I've yet to hear a good reason for taking children to watch drag queens or having children pose in pictures with high-powered rifles in their hands. However, those optics can be useful in antagonizing the other side. Many conservatives believe drag queens are immoral and progressives believe high-powered rifles are immoral, so there's no better way to offend them. These performative stunts are done to demonstrate how far we are from the values of the other side. That's the only purpose they effectively serve. I call this empty defiance.

Empty defiance isn't tied to anything morally good. It just signals our opposition to the norms and mores of the other side. It's provocation disconnected from virtue. The objective is merely to offend or enrage our opponents. It's driven by spite, not anything righteous. We're just trying to desecrate what the other side sees as sacred. In our opposition-centered stance, we're fine with our words and actions not serving any greater purpose. The civil rights movement's resistance was substantively pursuing God's will, whereas this kind of resistance is hollow.

When we center our rivals, we also tend to dismiss our wrongdoing by pointing out something worse on the other side. This often presents itself as "whataboutism," pointing out wrongdoing on the other side when confronted with your own error. Comparing our wrongdoing to a bigger error made by our opponents helps us avoid accountability. If conservatives are called out about racism, they say "what about" abortion. If progressives are called out about the poor state of many urban cities, they'll say "what about" conservative climate deniers. I've called this phenomenon "morality by comparison"—when our morality is relative to the actions of our rivals. We're never wrong because someone on the other side is doing something worse.

But that's not how morality works in God's economy. We're not right or righteous just because our opponent is more wrong. Judging ourselves based on the worst acts of others is moral folly and results in a wicked form of self-justification. That way of thinking creates a bottomless pit where our standards on both sides fall lower and lower. "We should not allow whataboutism to prevent self-examination and accountability."[27] Christians must evaluate themselves based on Christian principles and God's standards, not comparison to the sins of others.

As Christians, we have certain principles we must put into practice whether or not they serve our immediate self-interest or our side's narrative. Many of these principles—love, impartiality, honesty—are at odds with the culture-war mentality. Where rivalry causes bias and partiality by centering us and our narratives, the gospel compels us to evaluate things in truth and sincerity.

Jesus is the embodiment of Christian principles; our public witness must center on him. This replaces a spirit of tribalism with the fruit of the Spirit (Galatians 5:22-23). When Christ is at the center of our social action, spiteful, culture-war thinking is replaced with the principles in the Beatitudes, like a hunger and thirst for righteousness and peacemaking (Matthew 5:5-9). Vengeance is replaced with forgiveness, and winning political and cultural battles is no longer our primary objective. Those outcomes aren't unimportant, but they're preempted by our commitment to glorify God with our actions. As C. S. Lewis once said, "It is not your business to succeed (no one can be sure of that) but to do right: when you have done so, the rest lies with God."[28]

DISHONESTY

In our obsession with disproving, demonizing, and humiliating our opponents, facts and truth have become secondary at best. We've deprioritized the truth in pursuit of a perfect narrative that glorifies our teams. Whereas our storylines should be based on the facts, the facts end up being subject to our fixed ideological storylines. When a tragedy happens, we start with foregone conclusions about who was wrong and then cherry pick the facts that fit our conclusion.

For example, when there's a police shooting, some of us assume the police are right while others assume the police are wrong without even knowing the facts. Neither assertion is true in every instance, but they're often treated as if they are. We act as if knowing all the facts isn't necessary to make these determinations; they're just minor details. All we need is identities to insert into their storyline to arrive at a predetermined conclusion. Writer Bonnie Kristian points out, "We become certain about things that don't warrant certainty and doubtful about documented facts."[29] We also don't let the facts get in the way of us painting our cultural and political opponents in the worst light possible. They are as dumb, racist, or perverted as we say, and we won't accept anything to the contrary.

We're zealous in seeking to affirm our go-to storylines. This creates what philosopher Hannah Arendt called "a mixture of gullibility and cynicism." We listen to the influencers on our side with itching ears. We treat the other side's version with closed ears, hardened hearts, and little regard for the merits. As Arendt notes, we reach "the point where [we] will, at the same time, believe everything and nothing, think that everything was possible and that nothing was true."[30] Not only do we believe these things, but we also hurl accusations and condemnation at our opponents based on these fictions.

Instead of analyzing issues judiciously, our tribalism induces "politically motivated reasoning." Studies have found that "people use their minds to protect the groups to which they belong from grappling with uncomfortable truths. The motivation to conform is stronger than the motivation to be right."[31] In other words, we go to great lengths to make reality support our tribal narratives rather than dealing with facts that don't favor or flatter us. We tickle each other's ears to the point of becoming delusional.

Social media encourages dishonesty because users are incentivized by likes, retweets, and shares to put on dramatic performances and exaggerate to feed red meat to the bloodthirsty, online mob.[32] There's no reason to expect a thorough and intellectually honest conversation about serious issues. This has caused a credibility crisis. Credibility is currency in our democracy because people need to have a certain level of trust in you to be persuaded by you. But we've gone bankrupt on that account by dismissing inconvenient truths that are clear to the naked eye of any good-faith observer.[33] Every fact or reality that doesn't fit the Left's narrative is called a social construct, and every time someone brings up a historical fact that conflicts with our romanticized view of America they're called divisive. We're totally ill-equipped or unwilling to engage in honest debate. This makes solving issues such as police reform and racial injustices very difficult.

TO SAVE THE SOUL OF AMERICA

The SCLC, mentioned in chapter four, was the successor of the Fraternal Council of Negro Churches. Founded by Rev. Fred

Shuttlesworth, Dr. King, and others, it led some of the civil rights movement's greatest accomplishments. Sawyer explained, "The lifeblood of the SCLC was Baptist and Methodist and Pentecostal ministers and church members."[34] In a press release about the Montgomery bus boycott, the SCLC spoke on its organization's purpose:

> This conference is called because we have no moral choice, before God, but to delve deeper into the struggle—and to do so with greater reliance on non-violence and with greater unity, coordination, sharing and Christian understanding.[35]

As they saw it, this was part of being the church. By centering churches in their effort, "SCLC sought to frame the struggle for civil rights on moral terms."[36] Its signature achievements were the Civil Rights Act of 1965 and the Voting Rights Act of 1965. Unlike the culture war, to harm or disparage any other group was explicitly prohibited. They actually trained their volunteers about how to sustain verbal and physical assaults without retribution.[37] They were beaten and some were killed, but they refused to reciprocate the hate they received.[38]

The SCLC motto was "To save the soul of America," which is what both sides of the culture aspire to do in their own way, but they've centered the wrong things and many of their tactics aren't redemptive. Unlike the SCLC, they end up just trying to win the argument while being dishonest, spiteful, antagonistic, and destructive. They abandon their stated principles to gain an advantage.

The SCLC's refusal to reciprocate violence and vitriol was the product of a deep faith. They were trusting that God could overcome the lawlessness of the world without them resorting to the weapons of the world. Christians in the culture war have shown a lack of faith by imagining that insults and the dark arts of politics are necessary to achieve their objectives. Winning the culture war can't be at the center of our public witness, and spiting our opposition can't be at the center of our public witness. It must be centered on Christ. In the spirit of the Council, Christians can't allow rivalries, antagonism, and political and ideological labels to sever our commitment to applying Christian principles.

6

WE ARE SHARING

UPLIFT THROUGH PLURALISM AND CRITIQUE

We are sharing because the Lord's been good.

Rev. James Cleveland

FREDERICK DOUGLASS called the United States Constitution "a glorious liberty document" if taken "according to its plain reading."[1] Despite how it had been misinterpreted, he argued that it was the mechanism by which abolitionists would secure freedom for all men and women.[2] His faith told him freedom was God's design; and the Constitution was an instrument to obtain it in the here and now. It was neither perfect nor perfectly applied, but it was a great work of civic ingenuity. It is certainly not to be worshiped, but we'd be remiss to let its enormous potential go unrecognized.

That same grand instrument also contained the recipe to concoct a profound, if not unprecedented, ideal of civic pluralism. It established the framework and professed the ideals of a democracy with an open and inclusive public square—an arena that equalizes the voices of the powerful and powerless.[3] It wasn't to be merely the lecture hall of gilded oligarchs, the daydream of starry-eyed novices, or the landfill of raucous anarchists. In plain reading, it offered all a serious opportunity to be heard and to pursue a "more perfect union" through the equality and justice owed to all humanity. The American Experiment ambitiously sought to create a common objective among diverse races and beliefs without nullifying their significant theological and philosophical differences.

Sadly, the distance between those ideals and America's ability or willingness to do what was necessary to attain them have been massive. Not even the founders fully counted the cost of the self-sacrifice and transformation necessary to fulfill the words they wrote.[4] However, the potential and opportunity remain for those with enough moral imagination to continue the pursuit.

Mississippi Senator Hiram Revels, a Black preacher and the country's first Black US Senator, called out America's exclusionary laws and practices as an offense to God in a congressional address. He also proclaimed that one group's uplift wasn't dependent upon the degradation of another group:

> Prejudice has no cause to justify it . . . we must admit that it is wicked, we must admit that it is wrong; we must admit that it has no the approval of Heaven. Therefore, I hold it to be the duty of this nation to discourage it, simply because it is wicked, because it is wrong, because it is not approved of by Heaven. . . . this is the doctrine that I everywhere uttered: That while I was in favor of building up the colored race I was not in favor of tearing down the white race. Sir, the white race need not be harmed in order to build up the colored race.[5]

Willie Faye was the wife of a pastor. In the Black Church they're often referred to as the "first lady." It's a position of esteem and responsibility where the church is expected to treat her with reverence, and she's expected to behave with the utmost discretion and couth. To some extent, it was the closest thing Black America had to royalty, at least inside the church. As was often the case, the Black Church gave position and regard to Black people who were excluded and treated as less than in society. Street sweepers could be deacons and trustees in the church. In addition to being a first lady, Willie Faye was a lunch lady at a local school. Her race and position caused some to disregard her voice and right to be represented.

Sparked by the death of Dr. King, in 1968, many of the Black students at Decatur's Eisenhower High School staged a walk-out in protest of discrimination in the school. This included Willie Faye's sons, Tyrone and Dennis. They wanted more Black teachers and more fairness in the school's disciplinary process. Tyrone was an All-State football player and the school administration had urged his father not to let him participate in the protest because of his stature in the school. Willie Faye told her son to do what he thought was right and at a school hearing, she advocated for the administration to meet the protesters' demands. As she was speaking, one of the White male administrators told her husband to make her sit down. In response, Willie Faye indignantly, shouted, "He can't sit me down, only God can do that!" Notwithstanding her sex or class, God had given her a mind, a public witness, and agency, and she was determined to use them. In a small way, it was a demand for greater civic pluralism.

The Constitution sets a framework for civic pluralism, which is the recognition that we live in a diverse democracy, where people are free to speak their minds and live according to their convictions without intrusion. It recognizes that we were all created equal, have inalienable rights, and deserve representation. We have the right to share our perspective and opinions. It calls us to respect the beliefs of others and respect their right to disagree with us and challenge our most fundamental beliefs. Civic pluralism isn't just about respecting other people's right to disagree on issues we shrug off, but also protecting others' right to advocate for beliefs that contradict the core of our value systems and self-perceptions. We must protect the dignity and agency of others not only in disputes about how the national anthem should be sung, but also in conflicts regarding when life begins and how it should end.

It also requires a willingness to be proactive about working with others in good faith to do the hard work of democracy. We join hands to find common cause and compromise to identify solutions within our difference. It's the conviction that none of us are right or righteous enough to rule over others without their contribution. It's a commitment to be intellectually honest and self-sacrificial for the greater good. Democracy cannot survive without civic pluralism.

The civil rights movement, which was a Black Church initiative, was by virtue of its principles advocating for greater civil pluralism, as well as modeling it. They might not have used that language, but the compassion, respect, and intellectual humility they practiced are all values that produce and protect civil rights and civic pluralism. This was a Christian movement that by common grace learned from the teachings of Gandhi who was Hindu. Moreover, the March on Washington was civic pluralism in action. The organizers and speakers displayed an array of ethnicities and religious beliefs. A. Phillip Randolph, the march director, was an atheist.[6] Bayard Rustin, the march organizer, followed Quakerism, and two Jewish rabbis spoke at the event in addition to leaders from a number of Christian denominations.[7] While it was far from perfect, concerning the lack of women and disputes about Rustin, it demonstrated a spirit of civic pluralism that's profitable for us today.

THE NECESSITY OF CANDID CRITIQUE

Civic pluralism and critique are not mutually exclusive. Implicit in the call for civic pluralism is the existence of and need for critique. We are free to share our commendations and critiques of others. Civic pluralism sets the terms of engagement for that critique, but it doesn't neutralize it. Some have mistaken this concept to mean our disagreements will be less frequent and less stark or that we'll evolve to some enlightened cultural consensus on the toughest issues. That's a misconception of civic pluralism, and I'm not convinced the Right or Left have grasped this idea fully. Where some on the Right outright reject pluralism, the Left seems to think true pluralism inevitably leads to progressivism albeit in different flavors.

Civic pluralism shouldn't lead us into being so polite that we don't say what we mean or to pretend bad ideas are good. It's a commitment to seeking your neighbor's well-being and protecting them, not gratifying them. We have to promote respect and consideration for the beliefs of others without creating a sense of entitlement or encouraging hypersensitivity. Others should support our right to live, speak our minds, and flourish. We should invite each other in to seek understanding. However, no one is required to flatter us. Others can candidly question aspects of our culture without apology. They don't have to accept our arguments or pander to our eccentricities. They can frown on our tastes and opt out of our standards of beauty but should never impose theirs on us.

After all, this is the public square that St. Augustine and Aristotle paved, where legendary minds like Booker T. Washington and W. E. B. Dubois dueled. It's neither the ash tray of majority culture nor a playground where the thin skinned and their patrons enforce a tyranny of conformity. No person, culture, or movement is above or below critique. Atheists can call Christians shallow in frank terms but must never call our religious expression illegal. Muslims and Jews can offer honest critiques of one another without equivocation, but they must never question the other's unalienable rights. This is pluralism.

True civic pluralism isn't meant to create a nice and delicate public square. No, it should produce a more respectful and constructive space, where principles like equal representation and civility are mutually observed, but also where sincerity is still subject to proof and half-cocked arguments are taken to task. Pluralism shouldn't compel us to call a burglar a borrower, or a pimp a manager. The concepts we choose to normalize and legislate must survive a high level of scrutiny, as our lives and the future of this nation depend on it.

Treating dysfunction, immorality, and injustice with kid gloves is negligence not compassion. People shouldn't starve because prosecutors are too timid to apprehend the white-collar criminal. He must be prosecuted zealously and fairly under due process. Jesus was always loving and principled, but he didn't coddle (Matthew 15:21-28; 23; Luke 6:14-16; John 4:1-42). The truth must not be forced to stutter or condone a lie, but it can be articulated with grace and intellectually humility. We should sincerely be concerned about others' feelings while not allowing sentimentality to cripple the public discourse.

There are boundaries. Not all ideas or movements should be legitimized, but those lines are not to merely be drawn according to the moral preferences of elites. Highly credentialed citizens get to weigh in, but they don't get to exclude or dictate the values of the grassroots, even if they find them crude. The scope of pluralism can't be a short radius encircling elite consensus. That makes the public square and every value system the prisoner of polite society. That's not pluralism. If questions of economics or gender identity are still unsettled around the cafeterias of the common man, they must not be taken off the table by distant forces in the academy or corporate executives. One's degrees don't give them that authority and neither does one's populist "authenticity." We all have a say. The traditionalist and the reformer must have a seat at the pluralist table, otherwise it's counterfeit—a cover for classist or ideological intrusion.

Pluralism shouldn't be weaponized as a sword compelling timidity or assimilation, nor should it shield us from critique. There is no pluralism without deep difference and forthright critique. In this section, I will offer pointed critiques of conservatism and progressivism. I do so not to harm or humiliate either group, but because I sincerely believe some of their behaviors and propositions are destructive and harming people. There won't be any personal attacks, nor will I pretend my own tradition is faultless. I'll critique the Black Church tradition as well. I believe a civic pluralism that would silence such convictions is no pluralism at all. It's either a utopian fantasy or a front for ideological incursion.

We can disagree with someone's conclusions while acknowledging the good they've done, and that their intentions aren't always nefarious. For instance, I disagree with many evangelicals on racial justice, but I must acknowledge they give more to charity than other groups and their conviction regarding the sanctity of life implores them to take care of other people's children through foster care and adoption.[8] I also disagree with the progressive conception of truth, but that shouldn't keep me from recognizing the commitment to including marginalized groups throughout history. I continue to learn from both groups and believe they can learn from each other.

FAMILY BUSINESS

You've probably heard the term *family business.* It's the idea that certain information shouldn't be shared outside the family. There's a wisdom in keeping family business within the confines of close circles of trust, whether it's blood relations, ethnic groups, friends, or other communities and associations. If your brother wets the bed consistently or if part of your racial group lacks self-restraint in public spaces, there's discretion in not airing those issues out publicly. It's often a sign of grace, protection, and solidarity not to expose these problems with those who don't have the same commitment to your loved one's best interest. That said, this code of conduct isn't absolute, meaning it can lead to transgression in certain contexts. For one, it shouldn't cause us to deny the realities of our cultural pathologies, and every group has them. Second, it's this line of thinking that can lead to cover-ups and prohibitions on self-examination.

Some have gone so far as to suggest that if one critiques their own identity group, they're suffering from self-hate. I want to reject that assertion outright. It's absurd. Plus, anyone who spent time around Willie Fay and Mahalia's generation knows they had plenty in-group critiques that they preached from pulpits and discussed at dinner tables and in barbershops. These were not all private. The civil rights movement criticized the Black Power movement and vice versa.[9] The prohibition on examining your own group isn't part of the Black Church tradition, it's more so a culture-war trait.

In her book *Carved in Ebony*, writer Jasmine L. Holmes gives ten underappreciated Black female historical figures their flowers. One of those women was Nannie Helen Burroughs, who was a Christian standard bearer when it came to honor and dignity in the Black community. She was known for her piercing critiques of both White and Black people. Her contributions to her community gave her critiques credibility and reveal a spirit of edification. Her guidance was designed to improve people intellectually and morally. In analyzing Burroughs' commentary, Holmes described her as

> a thoroughly and consistent cultural commentator who cared enough about her Black Christian brethren to preach for their improvement, and who cared enough about her white Christian brethren to hold them accountable in those areas where improvement was limited due to ethnicity.[10]

When a loving and self-sacrificial family member sternly corrects us, we might be upset, but we can't claim they don't have our best interest in mind. Similarly, when Burroughs challenged men and women to act with self-respect, her love for them was undeniable. As Graves explains, "Her life's mission was to create opportunities for Black women in spaces where they scantily existed."[11]

Many of us have lost credibility in the public square because we're unwilling to honestly critique our own identity group. Our partiality taints our commentary and ensures others don't see us as good-faith actors. However, Burroughs didn't have any problem offering a candid critique of her community.

She wrote a piece entitled "Twelve Things Whites Must Stop Doing," which included, "Stop making unjust and discriminatory laws [and] molding social sentiment against respect for human personality . . . in an effort to prove the Negro is inferior."[12] This showed she deeply understood the oppression her people faced, but she also wrote "Twelve Things the Negro Must Do for Himself."[13] She recognized that her people, although oppressed, still had agency and she loved them enough not to let them waste it. She knew White America was the source of many of Black America's problems, but she also knew it wasn't honest or profitable to pretend we didn't need to do better in some respects. Culture war conservatives and progressives could learn from her example. Blaming everything on others is dishonest and disempowering.

In an American culture that's quick to take offense and slow to accept correction, her witness is worth remembering. It shows love isn't flattery or simply affirmation. Love can cause discomfort for the sake of pushing us toward personal transformation and uprightness. Our critiques must be an attempt to "speak the truth in love" (Ephesians 4:15). If humiliation is our goal rather than uplift, then we're doing it wrong.

Lastly, she wasn't an agent of outsiders, who critiqued her people to pander to others or for their entertainment. Burroughs was mostly speaking to her people for their benefit.[14] We should also avoid being the Christian that progressives have on call to criticize other Christians, or the Black person who conservatives have on call to criticize other Black people. The Bible instructs us to examine ourselves (2 Corinthians 13:5; Lamentations 3:40). The prophets publicly critiqued God's people for their own good (Amos 5–7). Refusing to do so leads us to confusion and disorder.

We also shouldn't shy away from others' fair critique of us. Our culture will lack self-awareness without such feedback from outsiders. In the spirit of Booker T. Washington and W. E. B. Dubois, Malcolm X and Dr. Martin Luther King, Zora Neale Hurston and Richard Wright, I will confront thinkers who I've learned from and might otherwise admire for the sake of cultural growth and civic pluralism, sincere and intentional misunderstanding come as it may.

7

AIN'T THAT GOOD NEWS

THE FLAWS OF CONSERVATISM

OVER A MILLION BLACK US military servicemen should've benefitted from the GI Bill when they returned from World War II. The low interest mortgages for homes would've greatly increased homeownership and generational wealth in the Black community. But as Black leaders pointed out, these soldiers had been fighting a double war—one for freedom abroad and one for justice at home.[1] The latter would be indefinitely delayed. Fearing Black veterans would take advantage of public sympathy for veterans to advocate for civil rights, Mississippi Congressman John Rankin worked to make sure the bill was administered by the states instead of the federal government.[2] A similar strategy was used in Franklin D. Roosevelt's New Deal to ensure fewer Black people received the benefits as states found old and innovative ways to deny them.[3] Two decades later, only 38 percent of Black families would own homes compared to 65 percent of White families.[4]

That episode in history certainly would've ended differently if the White American church, out of a sense of Christian compassion or patriotism, stood up against this grave injustice. In the Bible, the prophets Amos, Jeremiah, and Isaiah rebuked Israel for iniquity in the social context (Amos 5:4-12). However, those biblical principles weren't applied by many Christians to racial justice in America.

Here again, Black people often leaned on the Black Church when these issues arose. Prior to the Fair Housing Act of 1968, when White homeowners refused to sell to Willie Faye's family, they reached out to the Decatur Ministerial Alliance. This cross-denominational Black Church organization immediately used its social capital to pressure the homeowners to end their discriminatory practices and it worked. Around the same time, the SCLC was bringing awareness to housing segregation just north of them with its Chicago Freedom Movement.[5] When Mahalia Jackson moved into a White Chicago neighborhood, someone shot out her window in broad daylight.[6] The Black Church saw itself as a healer of spiritual and social brokenness. They believed they'd see "the goodness of the Lord in the land of the living" as God worked through their social action (Psalm 27:13).

LOVELESSNESS

In 1899, around two thousand White Georgians watched as Sam Hose, a Black man, was burned alive and subsequently had pieces of his organs and bones sold.[7] Later, ten thousand White Minnesotans attended the lynching of three Black circus workers. This happened far too often in the South, but also in the Midwest. They've been called "public spectacle lynchings," where White spectators viewed the extrajudicial murders of Black Americans in a celebratory fashion.[8] Regular churchgoers were a part of many of these White mobs—those who would call themselves Christians.[9]

First John 3:16 defines the Christian concept of love as self-sacrifice—laying "down our lives for our brothers and sisters." Under that biblical definition, White America and silent White churches displayed an indisputable lovelessness toward their Black neighbors. Public spectacle lynchings were the opposite of love. Yet, many conservative White Christians, like Pastor Henry Lyon Jr. of Montgomery, were defending white supremacy from a "Christian" perspective.[10] Only a few days after Freedom Riders were brutally attacked in Alabama in 1961, Lyon said,

> Ladies and gentlemen, for 15 years I have had the privilege of being pastor of a white Baptist church in this city . . . If we stand 100 years from now, it will still be a white church. I am a believer in a separation of the races, and I am none the less a Christian.[11]

By denouncing civil rights activists instead of racism and lynchings, Lyon and Christians like him, were doing the opposite of what God told Judean authorities to do through Jeremiah.

In Jeremiah 22, the prophet commanded them to "do what is just and right. Rescue from the hand of the oppressor the one who has been robbed" (v. 3). Lyons' words and actions can't be justified by the Bible, but historically, this lovelessness has too often been justified by those professing conservative ideology. Obviously, not all conservatives arrived at the same conclusions on race, but the prevalence of bigoted determinations reveals a brokenness in the ideology. Even if one can't say conservatism necessarily promotes racism and lovelessness, American history demonstrates that it often lacked sufficient principles or safeguards to prevent it. It's repeatedly been a seedbed for prejudice.

RECKONING WITH AMERICA'S PAST

Historian David Hollinger said, "Blacks, and blacks alone, inherit a multi-century legacy of group-specific enslavement and [group-specific individualized debasement] under constitutional authority in the United States."[12] Contrary to more convenient narratives, America's race problem isn't just a thing of the past; it still haunts us today. Black women are still "three times more likely to die from a pregnancy-related cause than white women,"[13] not just on account of socioeconomic factors, but because of American narratives and biases.[14] Bryan Stevenson points out that Black defendants are eleven times more likely than White defendants to receive the death penalty, twenty times more likely if the victim is White.[15] It takes some serious logical leaps and willful ignorance to separate those disparities from this country's long history of racism and from the American church's complicity.

Yet, according to Barna Group, less than half of White evangelicals agree that "historically, the U.S. has been oppressive to minorities."[16] They're rejecting objective historical facts. This is either blindness or bearing false witness. White Christians are also less willing to address racial justice than White Americans generally.[17] Such a dishonest and hostile public witness has robbed the church of moral credibility. If the cross of Christ doesn't cause us to humbly come to terms with our sin and publicly admit we, or the institutions we inherited, violated others then how can Christians reflect the good news we received? Many majority Christians have primarily responded to their failures on racial justice with willful blindness and defiance. In an all-consuming culture war, public humility is, apparently, too great a price to pay.

Pastor Vernon Johns spent nearly all of the 1950s negotiating with White preachers in the city of Baltimore about the role of the American church in times of racial tension. A significant part of his ministry at the Maryland Center was supported by White Baptist churches in the area as a missionary effort. But Johns wouldn't allow that relationship to prevent him from calling White Christian leaders out for their refusal to fully engage racial injustice in society.

At one meeting, Vernon created a very uncomfortable scene. Right after one of the White preachers finished a sermon that in no way challenged the status quo on racial justice, Johns stood up and rebuked him:

> The thing that disappoints me about the Southern white church is that it spends all of its time dealing with Jesus after

> the cross, instead of dealing with Jesus before the cross . . . That's all you hear. You don't hear so much about his three years of teaching that man's religion is revealed in the love of his fellow man . . . He who says he loves God and hates his fellow man is a liar, and the truth is not in him. That is what offended the leaders of Jesus's own establishment church as well as the colonial authorities from Rome. That's why they put him up there.[18]

The coalition of White and Black preachers would end shortly after those words and Pastor Johns would be asked to resign his position at the Maryland Center.

SPIRITUAL AWARENESS

In the Sermon on the Mount, Jesus preaches about the Christian focal point and perspective. Matthew 6:19-21 instructs us to store our treasure in heaven not on earth where moths and vermin destroy and thieves steal. Verses 22 and 23 use the metaphor of the eye as a lamp. The healthy eye shines light into the entire body and guides it in the proper way. Here, the eye symbolizes spiritual awareness or spiritual insight. This is our ability to perceive the truth—to see God's design, direction, and goodness clearly. This helps us determine what to treasure and what authority to serve. Conversely, a darkened eye leads to an unhealthy spiritual condition. This blurred vision causes us to value the wrong things and serve the wrong authority. The eyes of those in a healthy spiritual condition are watching God, who is the "light and salvation." They, in turn, as his reflection can be the light of the world.

The Black Church tradition of social action kept its aspirational posture by keeping its eyes on God and the good news of the gospel. The song "Keep Your Eyes on the Prize" was both an inspirational tune and a spiritual discipline. If the gospel was indeed good news, then they had to commit to overcoming fear and hate.

They had to deal with the dire reality without being overcome by it. Because their eyes were watching God, through the Black Church tradition of social engagement, Willie Fay and Mahalia's generation served as the light of the nation. They were strategic, but their faith pushed them beyond the X's and O's of game theory and the art of war.

Christians are most insightful, fruitful, and courageous when our eyes are watching God. Unfortunately, that viewpoint isn't prominent in Christian social engagement today. The culture war has shifted our focus and misplaced our treasure. For example, the Christian Right has won some victories and sat in seats of power, but on many accounts their eyes are averted and their treasures are earthbound. As a result, society isn't receiving light and inspiration from their engagement. Instead of being introduced to good news, our neighbors are witnessing characteristics attributed to other gods. There are Christians whose eyes seem to be watching Kratos, and his siblings, Nike and Bia. Kratos was the Greek god of strength, Nike was the god of victory, and Bia was the god of force, might, and compulsion. These gods are beheld and served at the expense of charity, grace, and neighborly self-sacrifice. They compel us to ask, who is my neighbor other than a political abstraction to be defeated?

Accordingly, when we listen to proponents of Christian nationalism, we don't hear worship of the God of justice and righteousness. We don't hear a faithful exposition of the gospel. We hear war jargon and verbal vengeance—a ringing gong and clanging cymbal exalting Kratos, Nike, and Bia. Here, the treasure is apparently in cultural domination, political power, and the humiliation of our opposition. It's an eye blinded by arrogance, lovelessness, and belligerence.

Above Kratos, Nike, and Bia, the American church stays in its culture-war posture because its eye is set on Hybris, who was the

Greek goddess of pride. In Roman mythology her name became hubris, which is an extreme or unreasonable sense of pride. It's thinking too highly of oneself. Those whose eyes are on the goddess Hybris are blind too. They're blind to racism and the sins of their own culture, but they can see everyone else's sin clearly. Their desire to be exceptional—seen as better than other people, better than other countries—has rendered them unable to see or acknowledge their faults and the consequences and implications thereof.

Many ideologically conservative Christians are engaging the public square with a darkened eye and in an unhealthy spiritual condition. Their public witness is failing to reflect the good news because it values political and cultural wins above justice and righteousness. Their religion is good news for them but bad news for cultural outsiders.

While progressivism is unable to accept certain facts of life, this conservative Christian was unable to accept historical facts. For many on the Christian right, American history and American exceptionalism have become an idol—a graven image of goodness and perfection to be secured at all costs. It's a shining, golden statue to which all Americans were obligated to bow in reverence. Apparently, this is where some conservative Christians find their identity and sense of importance.[19] According to this perspective, the American story puts us above other nations and we just need to return to the values of that hallowed era.

Idolatry always misdirects our eyes and misidentifies the location of our treasure. The only way to make something other than God seem faultless and worthy of worship is to distort reality. The historical facts must give way to the American myths that glorify the nation and its past. For some, talking about the history of American racism is the equivalent of a personal attack. This is why any mention of racial injustice in America must immediately be tied to Marxism and other nefarious, anti-Christian concepts. It can't be given a full hearing.

The impulse to look favorably upon the past isn't necessarily bad. Many cultures emphasize the best parts of their past, and this book is an example of that to an extent. Celebrating your culture's contributions can offer a healthy boost of our collective self-esteem and inspire greater works in the future. But we must be careful. We must remain truthful. Celebrating our past accomplishments can turn into downplaying or fully denying the not-so-flattering parts of our history. This is especially dangerous when that history is, in part, based on a sense of supremacy and when our denial keeps us from correcting ourselves. A romanticized view of American history has caused many White evangelicals to dismiss the just grievances of Black America and others and refuse to examine themselves faithfully.

Evangelical Pastor Robert Jeffress told his congregation America is a Christian nation, but "we allowed the liberals, the left, the progressives, the humanists, the atheists to pervert our Constitution into something the founders never intended it to be."[20] While Jeffress denied being a Christian nationalist and noted that any nation could be blessed by God, the storyline that America was righteous before the secular insurgence is historically inaccurate. It implies a golden age of morality where the nation was more closely following Jesus' instruction prior to the 1960s when racial discrimination was literally written in our laws or when Lost Cause Southerners massacred Black communities with impunity. This goes far beyond patriotism.

We can vigorously support our country without deifying it. We can celebrate the sacrifices of our forefathers without turning the US flag and the US Constitution into religious symbols. Former National Security Advisor General Michael Flynn even suggested that preachers need to be "talking about the Constitution from the pulpit as much as the Bible."[21] But the American Constitution is not the source of good news.

The truth is America has some exceptional achievements and ideals. Its innovations and generosity have greatly benefitted the world. The country also has some exceptional transgressions with some of its prosperity having come at the expense of others while its ideals have been at times null and void. Daughter of former slaves and co-founder of the National Association of Colored Women Mary Church Terrell noted, "The chasm between the principles upon which this Government was founded, in which it still professes to believe, and those which are daily practiced under the protection of the flag, yawn so wide and deep."[22]

Lastly, in some important ways, America isn't unique at all. We've fallen for the same temptations and impulse patterns that make all human history rhyme. Healthy eyes recognize these facts and healthy hearts are humbled by this reality. But the culture war mentality labels that recognition as treason and sees that humility as a sign of weakness. The Right has often allowed our successes to become arrogance and triumphalism and our failures to be revised and unspoken.

Arrogance can lure us into rationalizing our misdeeds like when Europeans convinced themselves they were helping the people they colonized. They were taking the Indigenous people's land and sovereignty for those people's "moral and material well-being."[23] This became a justification for western Europe's greedy and violent actions around the world.

Still today, diverse voices aren't valued in many majority churches. I wouldn't be surprised if most White evangelicals couldn't name a Black Christian theologian. Their churches only platform Black people who've fully assimilated into their culture. People from the Black Church tradition are presumed not to be theologically sound. Moreover, sociopolitically, many evangelicals will only cite Black people like Thomas Sowell and Voddie Baucham, who leave their failures on race unchallenged and even corroborate their most self-serving arguments.

This arrogance conflicts with Scripture, which says, "Do not keep talking so proudly or let your mouth speak such arrogance, for the Lord is a God who knows, and by him deeds are weighed" (1 Samuel 2:3). We tend to overestimate the value of our contributions and dismiss the contributions of others. The religious right's cultural perspective fits squarely in Dr. Martin Luther King's definition of racism, which he said is "the false and tragic notion that one particular group, one particular race, is responsible for all of the progress, all of the insights in the total flow of history."[24] Isn't this the spirit and message of Christian nationalism? It says, "Look at the nation my people created. You should be thankful, follow our lead, and shut up."

According to Georgetown Professor Paul D. Miller,

> Christian nationalism is the belief that the American nation is defined by Christianity, and that the government should take active steps to keep it that way. Popularly, Christian nationalists assert that America is and must remain a "Christian nation"—not merely as an observation about American history, but as a prescriptive program for what America must continue to be in the future. . . . Christian Nationalists do not reject the First Amendment and don't necessarily want a theocracy, but they do think Christianity should enjoy a privileged status in America.[25]

While America certainly had a strong Judeo-Christian influence, to say it was a Christian nation is an overstatement. Some of the founders were deists and many of the realities and practices of the country are and have been far from Christian. As Black journalist and anti-lynching advocate Ida B. Wells famously asked, "Why is mob murder permitted by a 'Christian nation'?"[26] She pronounced that the unpunished lynching of Black men was "a blight upon our nation, mocking our laws and disgracing our Christianity."[27]

Furthermore, Christian nationalism isn't all that Christian itself. Its proponents often push their cultural ideology and call it Christian. Historically, this ideology has been coupled with racism, hatred, and a lack of compassion. As a result, a lot of Bible-believing Christians in other communities wouldn't want to live under Christian nationalism any more than a non-believer because it doesn't accurately represent the faith.

Even if Christian nationalism were more Christian, it's not appropriate in a pluralistic society. Everyone's beliefs should be respected. My Muslim and atheist friends are no less entitled to express their ideas and try to mold the country in the way they think is best than a White evangelical is, and if their arguments are better, then they should win the day. Christian nationalism suggests that Christian conservatives are intelligent enough and benevolent enough to rule over others without their full contribution as citizens. As discussed in chapter 4, such a proposition cannot be defended from a historical perspective.

Again, such arrogance can't be justified within the Christian ethic. Furthermore, it's an arrogance lacking in self-awareness. Like a man parading around with an air of superiority while his fly is open and his toupee is off-center, many Christian conservatives are oblivious to how transparent their errors are and how little social capital they have in other circles. No one believes the good ol' boys are the all-knowing Good Samaritans of the world.

Yet, Christian nationalism has the audacity to imply that some Christian conservatives shouldn't have to do the hard work of democracy and persuade their neighbors. It's as if their authority should be assumed. They represent the ideological tradition that got slavery wrong and then opposed the civil rights movement. Under no circumstances should their judgment go unchecked.

Robert Jeffress says progressives ruined America, but some progressives sacrificed their lives for equality and justice while too many White evangelicals misused the Bible to defend injustice. Perhaps most ironic of all, the laws of the secular world had to force many conservative Christians to treat their brothers and sisters with human dignity. A people whose savior's greatest command was love had to be restrained by constitutional amendments, court injunctions, and National Guardsmen because they refused to "do justice" and "love mercy" on their own accord. Led by the Black Church, the progressives they condemn so fervently had to legally compel right-leaning Christians to acknowledge the human dignity of other Christians. There's plenty to be humble about.

As Frederick Douglass once said,

> But the church of this country is not only indifferent to the wrongs of the slave, it actually takes sides with the oppressors. It has made itself the bulwark of American slavery, and the shield of American slave-hunters. Many of its most eloquent Divines, who stand as the very lights of the church, have shamelessly given the sanction of religion and the Bible to the whole slave system.[28]

We could also say the American church was a bulwark of Jim Crow and of congregational segregation. The American church has done good works but has been an abject failure on racial justice. It's put forth little effort to fully reckon with that sin, let alone make amends.

The goal of Christian nationalism and the culture war generally is domination—to control the levers of society by dismantling the other side's institutions and rendering them powerless. It's an endless power struggle where Christians "rage" and "plot in vain" like the world as if God won't have the final say. This isn't only anti-democratic, it's not gospel-centered. While God's kingdom will reign, Jesus never told us to create a harsh theocracy, lord over others, and compel them into Christian values and practices. That's how the rulers of the gentiles conduct themselves, but Christians should be different. We should lead with good news.

If we want to become great, we must be servants (Matthew 20:25-26). Our love, service, and compassion are our primary tools in pursing the Great Commission, not compulsion. Compulsion doesn't inspire faith. No one truly and sincerely accepts Christ by having religion imposed upon them. Of course, we can promote laws restraining certain activity that directly violates the human dignity of our neighbors, but the Christian public witness should choose influence over domination. We do want to have a lasting impact on society, but not through the same force as Nebuchadnezzar and Herod. If we're imitating Jesus, people will be drawn to the gospel and not forced into cultural Christianity.

If Christians want the laws to better reflect our beliefs, then we must go persuade our neighbors. Help them understand why it's best for humanity in general. No group should have an assumption of rightness or any kind of privilege in the public discourse.

REFORM

Again, Christian conservatives have to reckon with the historical fact that their ideology got slavery and Jim Crow wrong. These consistent misjudgments had deadly costs for other image bearers and exposed a mechanical defect in conservative ideology. It revealed a severe malfunction that causes pride and callousness in its adherents. This glitch can desensitize and blind them to the pain of others. While some apologies have been issued, there's no indication that the religious right has fully taken responsibility for their sins of commission and omission. Those who have so much to say about personal responsibility have refused to hold themselves accountable.

Overall, White evangelicals have failed to establish the safeguards necessary to prevent their harshness from causing tragic misjudgments in the future. Getting things like American slavery and Jim Crow wrong should've caused a deliberate and massive overhaul of their ideological positions, but it hasn't. Many seem to have only done the minimum to avoid legal penalties and social sanction, which is insufficient to guard against the same offense happening in the future.

After the Titanic sunk, ships were redesigned by making their bulkhead higher and the bottoms were stretched to create double hulls. Also, the International Ice Patrol was established to monitor the presence and movement of icebergs at sea. Lastly, regulations were changed to make sure every vessel included enough lifeboat space for every person onboard. These deliberate precautions made the ships much safer on sea.

When something massively fails, you don't just assume it won't happen again without extraordinary efforts and guardrails. You do whatever is necessary to make sure it never happens again. White evangelicals must take these steps regarding race. The "get over it and move on" and "I didn't personally do it" disposition doesn't inspire confidence that they've truly reckoned with history and learned the necessary lessons. They must take the time to discover what's inherent about ideological conservatism that could cause them to get something so important so wrong.

We're told to stop talking about the past, but Jesus talked about the sins of the past because they were connected to the present circumstances. He reminded the Pharisees that their forefathers killed the prophets who they now claimed to be honoring by building fancy tombs (Luke 11:47). However, the Pharisees were also disobeying God and attacking the prophets of their day. What is it to honor the civil rights movement in word and then balk at cries for justice today?

In his play "The Tempest," Shakespeare says, "What's past is prologue."[29] In other words, history provides us with context for the present. The past tells us how we arrived at where we are. The chronological sequence of events offers insight into our current circumstances, and the Bible demonstrates this. Exodus and Numbers show us that later generations must restore what their forefathers misappropriated (Exodus 21–22; Numbers 5). The past doesn't necessarily dictate or justify future issues, but it certainly has a significant influence.

Its bigotry has also had generational consequences. How blind has Hybris made us? How great is her darkness that hides the impact of hundreds of years of slavery followed by Jim Crow, drugs flooding Black neighborhoods, and mass incarceration? Parts of the church deny the sins that haunt us in this age, even as massive racial disparities stare us in the face.

A JOINT FAILURE

Regrettably, one area where parts of the traditional Black Church have joined the religious right's errors is on the treatment of LGBT+ people. While the traditional Christian sexual ethic can't change, our lack of compassion toward our LGBT+ neighbors must change. We must approach these image bearers with a broken heart, one that laments all those who struggled with their sexual orientation and gender identity and were shamed or kicked out of churches with no extension of love, those who were given lessons about fire and brimstone condemnation but never told how much God loves them. If we're too prideful to apologize, we're too prideful to be faithful disciples. Historically, the American church has made an "us vs. them" fight out of something that affects all our families and churches. The "them" were always in our homes and churches and bore God's image.

While race and sexual orientation are different in important ways (and sexual behavior a different category altogether), the love imperative applies to how we should treat others. No one should be bullied or denied housing or banking because of their attractions and how they identify. We don't need to conflate love and affirmation of race and sexual orientation to protect our neighbors with tenacity and grace. Both the conservatism and progressivism have wrongly concluded that loving people means moral compromise. Now that we have seen how the Black Church social action tradition stands as a rebuke of the former, we turn our attention to the latter.

8

YOU WILL SURELY DRIFT AWAY

THE FLAWS OF PROGRESSIVISM

There's a storm out over the ocean and it's moving this way.
If your soul's not anchored in Jesus it will surely drift away . . .
It will surely drift away.

Michael L. Ross

THE CHRISTIAN CONSERVATIVE pursuit of power and refusal to fully reckon with injustice throughout American history has rightly drawn a lot of criticism as of late. Moreover, the habit of shaming others for personal sin while covering up institutional sins and denying the existence of systemic sin has created a reputation of open hypocrisy.[1] In some circles, conservatism is synonymous with hate and small-mindedness. Many young people and Christians of color are going out of their way to disassociate themselves with anything that could possibly be considered conservative. There's even a movement of "exvangelicals" or post-evangelicals who are loudly exiting the White evangelical church. They cite issues like racism, MAGA politics, and religious abuse as their reasons for rejecting that culture and sometimes the faith they grew up in.[2]

Since conservative ideologues in the church have deceptively used the Bible to justify historical wrongdoing, many have responded by the rejecting authority of Scripture too. They've mistakenly thrown the Bible out with the bad ideology and bad behavior. The American church's failure regarding justice were not due to them following the Bible too closely, but due to them not following the proclamations of Jesus, Isaiah, Jeremiah, and Amos closely enough.

Countless people are running from churches that seem more conservative than Christlike into the arms of progressive ideology. If conservatism represents hatred, hypocrisy, and an addiction to power, then its ideological opposite must be the answer, or so the reasoning goes. For those who are all too familiar with the harshness and anti-intellectualism plaguing parts of conservatism, progressivism presents itself as a compassionate and intelligent alternative. This conclusion is reinforced in popular culture, academia, and through corporate power. It's become a simple choice between love and hate, liberation and repression. Under that framing, progressivism is the obvious choice. One would have to be dimwitted or mean to think otherwise. However, the truth isn't so clear cut.

C. S. Lewis said that humanity rarely corrects errors of the past; we usually just end up making the opposite error.[3] For example, if our elders were too harsh on us as children, then we coddle our children. If they enforced burdensome standards of respectability, then we reject all standards of decency. If they unnecessarily demonized individual expression, then we make it god. This is our error. We've identified flaws in ideologically conservative Christianity but have overcorrected instead of making improvements.

The Black Church social action tradition drew a different conclusion. While disgusted by conservatism's rejection of social justice, the primary stream of the Black Church wasn't impressed by progressivism either. It often portrayed it as heretical concerning religious matters. Black Christian writers watching conservative and progressive religious thinkers battle during the 1920s "positioned themselves as the guardians of orthodoxy" and felt progressives had "left behind the foundation of Christianity." As historian Mary Beth Mathews put it, with conservatism condoning injustice, Black people were unsafe in the world; with progressivism's drift away from traditional Christian beliefs "they could gain the world but lose their soul."[4]

Where conservatism lacks compassion and an ability to fully reckon with our country's broken past, progressivism lacks moral knowledge and the capacity to reckon with human sin (outside of injustice) and inconvenient facts of life. Where conservatism insufficiently addresses lovelessness, progressivism enables a poisonous self-indulgence and confuses love with sentimentality. Secular progressivism has a superficial appeal because it responds to human desires and affirms their gratification, but it results in an incomplete public witness as it lacks the wisdom to see self-denial as a virtue. The Black Church tradition proves commitments to orthodoxy and social justice aren't mutually exclusive.

RACISM AND INJUSTICE AREN'T THE ONLY SINS

In James 1:25, the Bible calls the gospel "the perfect law that gives freedom." We're told not to simply listen to the gospel, but "do what it says" (James 1:23). It then informs the reader on how to faithfully put God's Word into practice: "Religion that God our Father accepts as pure and faultless is this: to look after orphans and widows in their distress and to keep oneself from being polluted by the world" (James 1:27).

Looking after orphans and widows is about demonstrating a self-sacrificial love when it comes to vulnerable people in our society. It's a matter of compassion and justice. Keeping oneself from being polluted by the world is about holiness and truth. We must uphold righteous standards that point toward God's design. It's a matter of conviction and moral order. One way to be polluted by the world is to adopt the world's values—to affirm what the Bible says is immoral or to treasure money and success over God and neighbor. We're not only commanded to work for the liberation of others, but also to be obedient and self-controlled ourselves. There's bondage in systemic sin and bondage in personal sin. This insight should lead Christians in our political and cultural engagement.

The Black Church social action tradition recognized that its efforts could become sinful if separated from God. The sin of injustice didn't justify every potential response. They were accountable for being holy themselves. The song "Lift Every Voice and Sing" (also known as the Black National Anthem) was clearly influenced by this ethic as the third stanza makes a prayerful request of God. Essentially, the lyrics wisely ask God not to leave his people to human devices. It says,

> Keep us forever in the path, we pray.
> Lest our feet stray from the places, our God, where we
> met Thee,
> Lest our hearts drunk with the wine of the world, we
> forget Thee.

This song, which reveals the connection between justice and God's will, also begs God not to leave us to our own conclusions, experiences, or to the influences surrounding us. It pleads with God to keep us from being intoxicated by the ways of the world. It confesses that our ways are not God's ways and we need God to keep us on the straight and narrow path. This is an acknowledgment that God is the source of our sobriety. If we're not anchored in the Word, we will surely drift away.

Mahalia Jackson was well aware of the evils of racism and systemic injustice in America. After all, she was the granddaughter of slaves and consistently felt the sting of discrimination in her personal and professional life, which is why she donated funds from some of her performances to the civil rights movement. She mentioned being confounded by the fact that Black women so often nurtured White children as nursemaids only to have White America show them brutality and contempt in return.[5] However, this didn't cause her to deny the sin in her community or in herself.

Mahalia grew up observing her father from afar. He had another family and apparently her existence complicated his other arrangement. As a young girl, she didn't have shoes to wear during an unusually cold winter in New Orleans. Eventually, she tearfully hunted her father down and asked if he would buy her shoes. He told her, "I don't have it; you better go," coldly rushing her away.[6] He was more worried about someone seeing them together than tending to the well-being of his motherless and shoeless daughter. Her cousin Celie said, she "never saw him give her a cent."[7]

Clearly, injustice wasn't the only sin that significantly impacted Mahalia's life. Her father's neglect had to hurt just as much, if not worse, than the hatred of a White stranger. An unfaithful husband would later bring Mahalia similar pain.[8] She acknowledged sin was not exclusive to White society when remembering how she had been cheated by White and Black promoters.[9] Those in any community who are self-indulgent hurt people around them, especially children.

Perhaps most importantly, amid all the pain brought by others, Mahalia recognized her own sin. After receiving a blessing from Pope John XXIII she reflected, "Lord, You cast seven devils out of Mary Magdalene. Maybe You can work some more on Halie?"[10] She didn't see herself as just a victim who needed to be liberated and affirmed, she was also a sinner who needed to be obedient to God's Word and personally transformed by the Holy Spirit.

Her life and her career weren't her own; they belonged to God. She saw gospel music as evangelism, not simply a means of self-expression. She constantly made it clear that she was a defender of the faith not just an entertainer, as anything less would be "a mockery to God's work."[11]

WEIRD VALUES

The attempt to make blackness and secular progressivism natural companions is one of the more dishonest narratives produced by the culture war. Traditionally, the Black Church's moral framework greatly contrasted with the ideological Left. Some social scientists have described the secular progressive ethic as WEIRD morals, an acronym that stands for Western, Educated, Industrialized, Rich, and Democratic. It has its origins and is still prevalent in Western countries like the Great Britain, France, and the United States.[12] Its current manifestation was primarily influenced by European philosophers like Nietzsche, Rousseau, and Hegel who explicitly rejected many of the Christian convictions—including faith and obedience to God. This value system is pervasive in elite universities, entertainment, mainstream media, and progressive politics.[13]

Unlike Willie Fay and Mahalia's community, which placed God at the core of their ethics, WEIRD values are based on an ethic of individual autonomy or self-rule. They assert that truth comes from within each individual rather than from an all-knowing God. Therefore, what's right or wrong is determined by the individual through the lens of their experience. Truth is not objective, certain, or necessarily the same for different people and cultures. When timeless, universal truths conflict with human feelings, desires, and perspectives, this value system assumes it's the truth that's broken. It assumes the individual is right, and when the Word of God or the facts of life don't affirm him, they must be deconstructed rather than acknowledged and accepted. In a way, it's a revolt against the facts of life.

Accordingly, individual expression as conveyed through speech, sexuality, and lifestyle trumps God's law and community standards. As expressed in every other Hollywood script, to remove oneself from religious restrictions, social sanctions, and community stigmas is one of life's greatest accomplishments. Therefore, anything that gets in the way of individual autonomy must be eliminated, whether it be religious institutions or an unwanted pregnancy. Finding yourself and living "your truth" replaces finding God and living according to his truth as the greatest good.

The only principle limiting the individual is that their expression can't hurt others. But in this analysis, determining whether others are negatively impacted is very shortsighted and often justified by consent. For instance, many secularists say prostitution is not immoral if all parties consent.[14] That ignores the deception, power differentials, and plainly unhealthy aspects of transactional sex. Many also say drug use is acceptable because it only affects the user. However, a more thorough examination reveals a serious impact on other individuals in the user's life, especially children, and society in general. In the Christian understanding, no third party is necessary for a wrong to occur. We defile ourselves and defy God when we don't act righteously, even if no one else's well-being is directly at stake.

Conversely, in songs like "Fix Me, Jesus" and "My Way Is Cloudy," the Black Church acknowledged we aren't naturally righteous or fit to lead our own way. They knew we needed a higher power because our perceptions and interpretations were flawed and would lead us to destruction. Our experiences and how we interpret them are not always reliable. They can cloud the true meaning of things. The "follow your heart" theme might be cute in Disney movies, but it's dangerous in real life. The Bible says,

"The heart is deceitful above all things" (Jeremiah 17:9). Our feelings and opinions can change from day to day, and we've all made earnest decisions that led to awful results. The value of autonomy ends where sin begins.

The fact that we don't have to lead our own way is good news. While the individual is precious and shouldn't be unduly restricted, we are also broken and in need of God and community. We need to be held accountable and edified. To be free without direction or a moral compass is quite simply to be lost. Even in a state of subjugation, the Black Church understood it wasn't only those who oppressed them who were capable of wickedness.

WEIRD values and true Christianity can't live inside the same human heart. We cannot serve two masters (Matthew 6:24-26). If we're devoted to secular progressivism, then we'll despise Christian principles when they conflict with our inclinations and plans. Ultimately, to accept WEIRD values you must reject the Christian concept of sin. Christianity doesn't make sense without the reality of sin because then there's no need for Christ. Our brokenness is just blamed on others. There's nothing we internally need to be saved from and we can all simply justify ourselves.

SIN AND A LACK OF MORAL KNOWLEDGE

Dr. Gardner C. Taylor addressed the WEIRD point of view decades ago in a sermon entitled "It Is Finished." He observed that many elites believe sin to be an "old, threadbare and outworn notion."[15] They believe it's obsolete and irrelevant to modern man. He conceded that the concept of sin was old and inconvenient, but he said the consequences of sin remain. The idea might fall on deaf ears in modernity. It might be dead to elites, but the ramifications of sin live on.

Dr. Taylor's point was that we still experience the results of sin, even if we're too highbrow or evolved to acknowledge its existence.

Intellectuals can ignore the unpleasant truth of sin, but none of us can escape its effects. Progressives might imagine life as happier when sexual sin and abortion are celebrated instead of discouraged, but the impact on society and the human soul don't disappear. We're not in control of this reality, no matter how much we think we know. Unlike in the movies, the small-town kid who leaves home for a life of self-indulgence in the big city can avoid his parents' rules, but he can't avoid the consequences if he chooses to break moral law.

Dorothy Day, a White, Catholic advocate, made a similar observation as she engaged with secular activists with WEIRD morals in the 1960s. They "preached liberation, freedom, and autonomy," as David Brooks explains in his book *The Road to Character*. However, Day wasn't impressed by that message. She proclaimed the value of the opposite: "obedience, servitude, and self-surrender."[16]

Day was not some naive pilgrim of piety. Earlier in life, she had been lax with her morality and more open sexually. Those actions resulted in a broken heart, a broken family, and an abortion. She grew wise enough to understand that there's nothing empowering about a lack of discipline and structure, which creates only dysfunction.[17] Day compared the radicals she worked with to adolescents who'd just discovered that their parents weren't perfect and, in a spirit of disillusionment, rebelled against all their instructions and institutions. "She'd say, 'All this rebellion makes me long for obedience' . . . Her colleagues' irreverent behavior demonstrated an immature and empty defiance that distracted from the work and weakened the movement."[18] Their lack of moral knowledge frustrated their social justice cause.

To Dorothy Day's point, at times, progressivism resembles the teenager who still doesn't understand why her parent's rules are necessary in the first place. She still thinks they're only enforced to oppress her when the boundaries are really in place for her own good, even though her parents are imperfect and may enforce the rules clumsily. In popular culture, her rebellion is seen as a virtuous evolution. We're left to pray that she discovers the truth before it's too late.

Some academics and the custodians of pop culture have found an alibi for every sin of self-indulgence. If it feels right, someone can find a way to rationalize it so we don't have to feel bad about our actions. But it doesn't matter how intellectual we are, sin still leads to suffering and death. Pleasure-seeking adults still lead to broken homes, broken communities, and broken children. Excess still leads to addiction and disease. Sin by any other name still has the same old results. We've become masters in euphemism. We can call prostitution sex work and adultery entanglement, but our new terms and descriptions don't change the age-old outcomes of sin.

Sadly, secular progressivism doesn't have the moral knowledge to reconcile that truth. Speaking the truth on these issues is characterized as closed-minded, mean, and judgmental. And the truth is the church has been some of those things in the past, but there is a way to speak the truth in love. The Black Church tradition recognized humans aren't the center of the universe and the truth isn't ours to create.

In Isaiah 55:9, God tells us, "As the heavens are higher than the earth, so are my ways higher than your ways and my thoughts than your thoughts." This is hard for the secularized mind to accept, but when our desires and intellectual conclusions conflict with the Word of God, this passage gives us the reason why that's too often the case. We shouldn't "pervert the grace of our God into a license for immorality" (Jude 4).

As we acquire more education and credentials, some of us are actually lured away from moral knowledge, wisdom and, at times, even common sense. It is possible to consume more information without growing in moral knowledge. For instance, someone else can know little about biology, empirically speaking, yet comprehend why even unborn life has value. The best-case scenario is to have both, but it's incorrect to assume book smarts are indicative of a wealth of moral knowledge.

This could mean Granny, who didn't finish high school, has the equivalent of a PhD in moral knowledge while your Ivy League sociology professor needs to go back to children's church for remedial instruction. Understanding this reality can help us delineate between different kinds of knowledge. Christians must have the discernment to accept the empirical data while spitting out the unsound moral teachings.

"He ain't got good sense." Anyone who spent time around Willie Fay and Mahalia's generation heard this phrase from time to time. It means someone lacks common sense and it isn't reserved for those who are uneducated. We all know people who are "book smart" but lacking when it comes to understanding other daily life matters. Overthinking and thinking from a false premise complicate simple truths. There are certain things people can take for granted because they're obvious.

For example, as a general matter, men are physically stronger than women.[19] For centuries, cultures all over the world have accepted this fact. It's rightly reflected in criminal law and is part of the basis of Title IX's equal opportunity language. We must be careful not to overstate that fact or draw bad conclusions from it, but the fact exists whether we like it or not. Recognizing the difference between biological sexes allows us to be more just. Both sexes have certain limitations placed on them by nature. Conversely, denying this fact through convoluted theories and circular arguments only erodes one of the most practical guides we have—common sense. We need common sense to make good policy and protect people.

UNDUE INFLUENCE

While there have certainly been White progressives who've been respectful and self-sacrificial toward Black America, Black leaders have long suspected that some were using us and our issues as pawns in their rivalry with conservatives. Congressman and pastor Adam Clayton Powell felt the Left attempted to assert an undue influence over Black leaders and movements. He went so far as to say that they tried to choose our leaders for us by only giving exposure and support to those who cosigned their ideology and were preapproved.[20]

Christian journalist Ida B. Wells, who led an anti-lynching crusade in the United States, also noted the vain motives behind the antics of some race "allies."[21] She perceived some White people seemed to be inordinately or performatively courteous to her primarily to shock other White people in the vicinity.[22] She felt she was being used to provide leftists opportunity to virtue signal and further distinguish themselves from conservatives.

The Black Church social action tradition has had many genuine progressive partners from the majority community, but some of their participation in the race conversation has been self-interested. It's also been motivated by a type of savior complex. Author Zora Neale Hurston facetiously called them "Negrotarians"—an obvious play on the word *humanitarian* but describing those who fashioned themselves as saviors of the Black race.[23] In an article entitled "The Great Awokening," writer Matt Yglesias cited a study showing that on race issues "white liberals' opinion has moved to the left of where black and Latino opinions are."[24] It's hard to make sense of why this would be the case unless other motives are at play.

In institutions of higher learning, in a kind of formation process, Black students are rewarded for focusing almost solely on race and targeting conservatism. In his memoir, *How Far to the Promised*

Land, Dr. Esau McCaulley describes his experience with this dynamic in college:

> For all my talk of rebellion, I had been formed into exactly what some at Sewanee (University) wanted me to be: a Black intellectual who took the progressive side in all-white conversations about politics and theology. Stated differently, my professors and classmates wanted Black people to call out racism and critique the system, and that was about it. They needed Black voices to challenge their enemies on the right: they needed their critiques dipped in chocolate. That was our role on campus. Even my rebellion felt scripted. I needed to find a distinctively Black and Christian way of being. I needed less Bertrand Russell and more Frederick Douglass.[25]

Unfortunately, not all of us are blessed to have Dr. McCaulley's epiphany. If our public witness only talks about race, it might not be as "authentic" as it seems. The Black prophetic tradition has always called out racism and Christians, in general, should continue to do so. However, undue influence has been placed upon Black leaders and movements to limit our public witness to race and remain silent on any number of issues that may call progressive ideas and institutions into question. We've been disincentivized and discouraged from calling out progressivism's lack of moral knowledge.

To some extent, this dynamic has caused a disconnection between the leadership class and common people in parts of the Black Church. On the tough issues, the Christian leadership class often fails to stand on orthodox Christian principles in the public square. This includes those in the Black Church and in other communities. According to a 2023 Pew Research Center poll, while most Black people believe we should compassionately address the issues LGBT+ people face, almost 70 percent of Black people say that whether a person is a man or woman is determined by one's biological sex.[26] That number increases to 84 percent for Black adults who attend religious services once a week.[27] The "Black delegation" has spoken and said, "We care about our LGBT+ neighbors, who are made in the image of God, but the truth is gender is binary and manhood and womanhood are biological." Yet, in an urban center like Atlanta, Washington, DC, or Chicago, you'd be hard pressed to find a politician who'd ever publicly represent that nuanced position.

The case was similar with the Defund the Police movement. Based on the coverage and the position of many influencers, one was led to believe most Black people supported the effort.[28] However, over 81 percent of Black people said they don't want less of a police presence in their areas and only of 22 percent supported abolishing police departments.[29] Most Black people wanted police reform that led to better treatment rather than the senseless extreme of reducing the police presence in high crime areas.[30] Curiously, our representatives often advocate for the furthest leftward position in the public square.[31] Some Far-Left groups seem to manipulate the importance of representation and launder their agenda through the Black struggle. In order to please the donor class, many well-intended leaders are caught up in a culture war framework that their pewmates don't espouse.

Regrettably, many of the prominent voices in the leadership/professional class fall into two categories: those who've sincerely come to believe almost all secular progressivism's social tenets and those who have significant disagreements with the Left on social issues but who have chosen self-censorship based on a sort of career cost-benefit analysis. In other words, those who've been indoctrinated and those who just go along to get along. Christians who fit into either group have severely compromised their public witness.

INDOCTRINATION—BEING DISCIPLED BY SECULAR PROGRESSIVISM

Christians in the professional world and leadership class who promote some of the most extreme parts of the secular progressive agenda don't do so randomly but based on a system of influences and incentives. Most American Christians have been heavily exposed to the influence of popular culture by the time they reach adulthood. Through media, music, and the educational system, we're presented with secular worldviews and norms ad nauseam. It's on Nickelodeon and in Disney songs. It's in our textbooks, in our conversations with peers, and now on social media feeds. This is to be expected when you live in a culturally diverse nation where people have different values, and it isn't necessarily bad. We can and should learn from others and contribute to the good of larger society. However, we also know the values of secular society often conflict with the tenets of the church, and if we're not careful, society will influence us more than we influence it and can begin to control our public witness. For example, as Christian leader Dr. Gabriel Salguero points out, Latinos become more secularized the longer they live in the United States.[32]

Charles Taylor noted that we live at a time where faith in God is one option among many, and today, pop culture's view of religion is rooted in the secularization hypothesis. This idea says, "Societies outgrow religion as they modernize."[33] In other words, religion is eventually recognized to be nothing more than superstition and fades away as science and technology develop. Ultimately, we become too intelligent and self-sufficient to believe in the myths that preoccupied our ancestors.

This was the theme of comedian Bill Maher's documentary film *Religulous*, where he goes around the world mocking religion. At the end of the documentary, Maher says this:

> The plain fact is, religion must die for mankind to live. The hour is getting very late to be able to indulge in having key decisions made by religious people . . . This is why rational people, anti-religionists, must end their timidity and come out of the closet and assert themselves. And those who consider themselves only moderately religious really need to look in the mirror and realize that the solace and comfort that religion brings you actually comes at a terrible price.[34]

Maher's monologue is a candid version of the progressive culture war position that's present in popular culture and academia. If most American Christians have received a significant dose of this secularization hypothesis, then the Christian professional class has been exposed to it like radiation after the Chernobyl nuclear plant explosion. We've been swimming in the contamination for years and now have a florescent green glow illuminating our skin. If this were a nineties cartoon, we'd have grown extra limbs and become mutants with superpowers. It's so prevalent around us that it's begun to feel instinctive.

When many of us entered college, the secularization hypothesis doused our faith with cold water, leaving us lukewarm. We've become the moderately religious people Maher urged to take the leap into full disbelief. We indecisively stand at the edge of the plank. We were sent to college to write better, solve more complicated equations, and better understand the sciences, history, economics, and philosophy. We were then expected to apply those skills to better our communities. However, in academia, we also acquired a substantial amount of ideological indoctrination. There was a deliberate effort to replace our biblical values with a secular progressive alternative.

If I hadn't experienced it myself, I'd probably think it was just another conservative, tinfoil hat conspiracy. A 2017 study found that "60% of the faculty identified as either far left or liberal compared to just 12% being conservative or far right."[35] It's not just Christians who are concerned about the leftward bias in higher education. Non-conservative, non-Christian thinkers like lesbian writer Bari Weiss have been sounding the alarm to expose the problem. Now, even Bill Maher thinks progressive indoctrination has gone too far.[36] He says the culture war left is "pushing indoctrination in classrooms" before college too.[37] As a result, we don't just get knowledge and skills, many of us get a new worldview and a sort of moral miseducation at odds with our faith tradition.

Impostor syndrome and accompanying insecurities caused us to seek validation within the academic environment. In lecture halls, esteemed scholars stand before us. Their vocabularies are grand and intimidating. They grade our examinations based on the books they and their peers wrote. The obvious conclusion is their word is to be revered and learning often entails imitating their manner, language, and ideological bent. Surely, they know more about the purpose of life and sexuality than Auntie and Deacon Junebug back home. In college we get a package deal of empirical knowledge and a new system of belief (or unbelief), and few of us are able to distinguish between the two. In many institutions of higher learning, conforming to the culture is a sign of high aptitude and a rite of passage into a more enlightened space.

The clearest indicator of our indoctrination is that we've come to believe progressivism is almost synonymous with intelligence and sophistication. In other words, we think the more you know, the less traditional and more progressive you become. We see progressivism as a sign of refinement and accomplishment. We've bought into the idea that intellectual curiosity and attainment naturally lead to secular progressive thinking. This misconception has a massive influence on our beliefs and aspirations. Through this process, Christians are being discipled by progressive ideology.

I've been surprised by how willing Christian academics and activists are to let secular progressives frame the issues for them, determine the language, and set the terms of engagement. This has significantly diminished any unique contribution the Christian Left could be making in the public square. It often seems like they're confined to imitating, translating, and repeating. But the truth is progressivism is very limited because it denies absolute truth and can't accept the reality of sin. Therefore, progressivism can't even articulate the origin of the justice it claims to hold dear.

If there's no absolute truth and everyone decides what's right and wrong for themselves, how can we compel anyone to treat others justly? To demand justice is to invoke a timeless, universal, and unconditional standard that applies to everyone regardless of their cultural assumptions and preferences. It says that every human being has value that must be respected. That's a statement of absolute truth. To set a standard of justice that always applies to everyone, regardless of their own beliefs, requires us to recognize that human dignity is inalienable and absolutely true. In other words, the human dignity of every race stands whether the white supremacist believes it or not because truth isn't determined by his beliefs or his culture. It's above and beyond him. That's good news, and Willie Faye and Mahalia's generation knew it, even when the human authorities who oppressed them said otherwise.

AMBITION MEETS CANCEL CULTURE

"Where you have envy and selfish ambition, there you find disorder and every evil practice" (James 3:16). The errors of progressivism have run wild not just because of those who are indoctrinated, but also because of those who know better but are afraid to speak the truth. Not every non-conservative person believes biological men playing women's sports makes sense, but few will say it publicly, especially in the professional and leadership class where many fear their career prospects will be limited if they speak out against the ideological Left's agenda. If our ambition isn't guided by principle, it'll be guided by opportunity and fear. This is what the Bible refers to as selfish ambition—making our needs and desires a priority over biblical tenets like speaking the truth (Galatians 5:16-17). Going along to get along makes us cowards in the public square. If a Christian isn't firm in their conviction, when cancel culture is in the vicinity, they will surely drift away.

There are real consequences to pushing back on the Left's view of abortion, sexuality, and gender identity. As designed, those consequences have altered the cost-benefit analysis of many ambitious Christians who've decided it's best not to rock the boat. As Dungeon family poet Big Rube once said, we've become "cowardly lions never defying the jackals of Babel."[38] We lack backbone. Even in the pulpit, some are unwilling to push back progressive narratives.[39] Cancel culture has censored social critiques of the Left.[40] It tarnishes reputations and forecloses opportunities. This is a cause for concern for all of us, but it's the worst-case scenario for those serving the idol of careerism. When professional achievement is our first objective, we're quick to surrender our values.

The father of progressive activism, Saul Alinsky, detailed the Left's cancel cultural tactics decades ago. When dealing with a political opponent, he said you must:

> Pick the target, freeze it, personalize it, and polarize it. Cut off the support network and isolate the target from sympathy. Go after people and not institutions; people hurt faster than institutions. (This is cruel, but very effective. Direct, personalized criticism and ridicule works.)

The ideological Left is very effective at identifying, isolating, and demonizing people who disagree with them. Many progressive activists claim to be aligned with the spirit of the civil rights movement, but these tactics more so resemble the efforts of the White Citizens Counsel from the 1950s and 1960s. The WCC was a Southern business class organization that terrorized Black people through the law, politics, and economic retaliation to maintain segregation. They presented themselves as being above the Ku Klux Klan's violent tactics, pretending to be upstanding by practicing "all legal means." For example, they'd pressure businesses to fire employees who spoke out against Jim Crow. This had the effect of "suspending free speech" about integration in some areas. Writer David Halberstam said, the WCC used "respectable means for unrespectable ends," which is why some called them "manicured Ku Kluxers."[41]

The Black Christian tradition stood up against this type of treatment—they didn't engage in it. Maliciously attacking your people with deceptive and cruel tactics for disagreement in the public square is outside of the Black Church tradition's "love your enemies" ethic. They were tenacious in combatting injustice, but becoming evil to fight evil wasn't acceptable. While they've fashioned themselves as the compassionate side, the ideological Left still has a lot to learn in that regard.

Christians have been caricatured as closeminded, bigoted, and hypocritical. That's been a theme in popular culture and polite society for some time and a source of intense ridicule. Alinsky spoke on the efficacy of ridicule too, "Ridicule is man's most potent weapon. It is almost impossible to counterattack ridicule. Also, it infuriates the opposition, who then react to your advantage."[42] Anyone who's listened to a Dr. Gardner C. Taylor sermon or read the poems of Phyllis Wheatley knows not all Bible-believing Christian are closed-minded, bigoted, and hypocritical, but this narrative has caused an inferiority complex in some Christians. They now go out of their way to escape the stereotype by constantly trying to prove how progressive they are to their peers. In some cases, we're ashamed of the gospel and become simps and sycophants to fit into secular society.

We repeat the Left's language and systems without any sign of critical analysis. We've sadly become echoes—delighted with getting a pat on the back for adjusting Christian principles to fit progressive conclusions and cosigning the Left's latest social constructs no matter how extreme. If you want to know what we'll claim next, you'd be better off asking secular progressives than asking us. We've outsourced our public witness such that it's practically and substantively indistinguishable from secular progressivism. This has gutted what's authentically Christian from our public witness.

Some Christian leaders seem to be pursuing a sort of inverted Great Commission, turning it inside out. Instead of going from the church into the world to make disciples, we've come out of universities like Vanderbilt, Duke, and Emory back into the church to make secular disciples in the church. Convinced the church is backwards and irrelevant, many of us have endeavored to modernize it morally. We seek to update our congregations with the latest progressive language, systems, and moral perspectives like apps and bugs fixes on an iPhone. Making sure the church is addressing society effectively is a good thing, but changing the church's timeless teachings to conform to the world is not.

There are many things the church must improve, but how we define improvement matters. Is the objective to put a Jesus piece on progressivism and call it Christian? We cannot be leaders in the church but followers outside the church. We can't lead while longing for validation from secular influencers, activists, and academics. The objective of Christian leaders can't be to either keep the church from changing at all or to make the church as ideologically progressive as possible—legalism or apostacy. Like Wille Faye and Mahalia's generation, we must lead with confidence and humility—confidence in the Word of God and humility concerning your broken self.

9

I KNOW THE LORD WILL MAKE A WAY

MORAL IMAGINATION

You can live weeks without food, days without water, but only minutes without hope.

Dr. Frank E. Ray Sr.

THE ESSENCE OF BLACK AMERICAN expression has often been referred to as "soul." It's the sensibility that inspires our oratory, music, and lingo. It's the flavor that seasoned Dr. Gardner C. Taylor's sermons and it's the shout in Mahalia's praise. Soul can't be fully described because it's a feeling. It's not mine to give to you, but I can show you. In the church—at its purest—it's a spiritual connection with God who's uniquely inspired every group of people in some special way. Theologically, soul is related to how we perceive things, and it shapes human personality and style (Matthew 16:26; Luke 9:25).

Perhaps no pen was ever more soulful than that of Dr. Charles Tindley, the son of a slave and known as the "Prince of Preachers," credited with being one of the creators of gospel music.[1] His song "I'll Overcome Someday" captures the spirit of the Black Church social action tradition's vision and steadfastness:

This world is one great battlefield,
With forces all arrayed;

If in my heart I do not yield
I'll overcome some day.
I'll overcome some day,
I'll overcome some day;
If in my heart I do not yield
I'll overcome some day.[2]

Decades later, those words would hearten civil rights advocates when transformed into the spiritual "We Shall Overcome."[3] That song would become the definitive expression of those who considered themselves the "conscience of America."

We shall overcome, we shall overcome,
we shall overcome someday!
Oh, deep in my heart
I do believe
we shall overcome someday![4]

One of the most important aspects of the soul of any person is not swagger or any type of oratorical style, but rather the moral imagination at the core of their view of the world. It's the motive for a people's perseverance and the vision inspiriting their hope. Historian Andrew Manis said, "African American spirituality looks disappointment and despair and death in the face and declares that beyond all these there is hope."[5]

Dr. Tindley's life is an example of Romans 8:24-25—hoping and believing in what you do not yet have based on God's promises. One historian noted that rather than making him bitter, his oppressed and impoverished childhood "taught him a deep faith" and gave him a sense of gratitude.[6] That's a decision based on a core conviction about who God is. It's the Holy Spirit informing the soul that it can transcend its current circumstances.

Tindley's moral imagination shone not only through his song lyrics, but also in his public witness. He was a pastor and community leader who opened a soup kitchen and advocated against minstrel shows that denigrated his people.[7] His gospel-centered outlook deliberately chose hope over bitterness and despair. It's not wealth nor social status that determine whether we'll live in bitterness or not. King Herod was bitter while Mary, a poor Nazarite, sang a hymn of praise and gratitude in Luke 1:46-55. It's our moral imagination—the hope we employ as we interpret our experiences, set our expectation, and order our passions—that determines that disposition.

There are times when despair is an understandable emotion given a bleak reality and a history of recurring pain. Even Dr. King despaired after his civil rights initiative failed in Albany, Georgia, in 1961.[8] The city reneged on their agreement to release protesters on bail, SNCC leaders criticized his involvement, and news reports called it "one of the most stunning defeats in King's career."[9] There are moments when hopelessness is a reasonable conclusion based on a thorough survey of the material circumstances.

However, for Willie Fay and Mahalia's generation, the analysis could never end there. What they could see physically or observe through recent history was only part of the equation. What they had experienced and believed supernaturally also held sway and was just as real as the history of pain. Hopelessness and despair were understandable based on what they were living through. They were all too familiar with Black America's bitter plight. Yet, they believed wallowing in hopelessness and despair was unwise, unfaithful, and to be avoided at all costs.

The Bible gave them reason to believe better was not only possible, but in store. It revealed God's intentions: "Behold, I am doing a new thing; now it springs forth, do you not perceive it? I will make a way in the wilderness and rivers in the desert" (Isaiah 43:19 ESV). Based on this understanding, generations of Black churchgoers confidently sang, "I know the Lord will make a way . . . oh yes, he will" with vigor and expectation. We perceived that truth through our moral imagination.

Moral imagination is the ability to see not simply what has been historically, what is in the present moment, or what's likely to be in the future. It's the ability to see what ought to be and what will be based on God's capacity, character, and promises. God is all powerful—his capacity is endless (Psalm 115:3; Isaiah 55:11; Jeremiah 32:17). God has promised to strengthen us, end all suffering and death, and to never leave us if we believe in him—his promises are sufficient and eternal (Deuteronomy 31:8; Isaiah 41:10; Revelation 21:3-7). This compassionate, all-powerful God who wants relationship with us and is moved to compassion by the groans of the afflicted and oppressed was the foundation of the moral imagination that led Willie Fay and Mahalia's generation (Judges 2:18). Reason and emotion alone can't apprehend the gospel ethic. Both are useful tools as we endeavor to understand our world and express ourselves, but they are limited and insufficient for a fuller redemption and flourishing in the moment and beyond. A faithful witness requires moral imagination since "we live by faith, not by sight" (2 Corinthians 5:7).

When faced with long-lasting, brutal injustice, we have a few general choices: accept our subjugation as unchangeable, deny reality and live in escapism, or acknowledge the present reality while seeking to overcome and fundamentally change it. Many have chosen the fatalistic approach. To some extent, they dispiritedly accept certain obstacles as immovable and certain powers as invincible. This perspective is masterfully illustrated in the classic movie *The Wiz*, a Black cinema adaptation of L. Frank Baum's *The Wizard of Oz*. In one of the opening scenes, the Scarecrow (Michael Jackson) is surrounded by a flock of cynical crows who seem to enjoy mocking and discouraging him, as they say misery loves company.

He's told he'll never be free from the oppressive, cruciform pole he's been hanging from his entire life. They even make him sing a song, "The Crow Anthem," to reinforce the pessimism they're determined to implant in him:

> You can't win, you can't break even
> And you can't get out of the game
> People keep saying things are going to change
> But they look just like they're staying the same . . .
> You can't win, child
> You can't break even
> And you can't get out of the game.[10]

Based on the crows' experience, such a dreary view of their world might've been, in a sense, well-grounded and perhaps substantiated by the hard data, but the Scarecrow was different. He had moral imagination, which eventually allowed him to "ease on down" the yellow brick road and accomplish things he could've never otherwise foreseen.

Through the years, when it comes to social justice, we've seen some of our most talented influencers repeat a version of "The Crow Anthem" that America has bludgeoned Black people into reciting. White supremacy has been depicted as the natural order or as too powerful and ubiquitous to defeat. After hundreds of years of slavery, Jim Crow, and so on, it's understandable that some would succumb to this perspective, but it's less faithful and fruitful.

From the White mob violence during Reconstruction to the burning down of Black Wall St. in Tulsa, Oklahoma, the message was clear: "Give up! Things will never get better." Regrettably, we saw this reflected in Black legal scholar Derrick Bell's thoughts on the permanence and indestructability of racism. He contended that "racial equality is, in fact, not a realistic goal."[11] It's one thing to say racism is deeply embedded in our society. It's quite another to say it's invincible.

Bell goes on to say that when it comes to race all progress is temporary and setbacks are inevitable. We're resigned to mitigate the damages of white supremacy and pursuing the goal of defiance by harassing White folks.[12] To be fair, Bell wasn't arguing for Black people to just give up, but his downbeat perspective erroneously sets the bar so low that it can't inspire hope or perseverance. The likely result is a bitter and vengeful spirit. That's no way to live.

In Ta-Nahisi Coates' award-winning book *Between the World and Me*, he writes to his son about America's history of racism:

> You must struggle to truly remember this past in all its nuance, error, and humanity. You must resist the common urge toward the comforting narrative of divine law, toward fairy tales that imply some irrepressible justice . . . Perhaps struggle is all we have because the god of history is an atheist, and nothing about this world is meant to be. So you must wake up every morning knowing that no promise is unbreakable, least of all the promise of waking up at all. This is not despair. These are the preferences of the universe itself: verbs over nouns, actions over states, struggle over hope.

This is indeed despair—an ode to cynicism justified by a god who's aloof or completely non-existent. He believes the most we can strive toward is a life of "interrogation and struggle."[13] With his impeccable pen and rhetorical flair, Coates gives one the feeling this is the height of racial awareness. His letter suggests once we reach the peak of our intellectual interrogation of race in America, we find our fate sealed as faces at the bottom of the well in perpetuity.

The works of Bell and Coates are far from being without merit. They've added much to the discourse on race, but here they are wrong and dangerous. Dr. Gardner C. Taylor once explained that to say God can't change a situation is "to impeach the authority of God" and who would dare "stand in the presence of the Eternal and cast a pall of doubt over what he can do."[14] It's doubleminded for a Christian to find no objection in Coates' at best dryly agnostic train of thought.

As noted by Brown University professor Dr. Melvin L. Rogers, Coates is said to be the successor of James Baldwin, but he missed one of Baldwin's most important insights, which was Black folks "can't afford despair."[15] Struggle, interrogation, and harassment are not sustenance. God-inspired hope is a life source. It doesn't just make life survivable, but meaningful and beautiful. Coates couldn't offer his son hope, but Baldwin explicitly forbade passing that cynical conclusion on generationally.[16] It's communal malpractice.

I find it odd Coates couldn't encourage his son to be hopeful by the collective impact and reach of his father's voice. Could he not find comfort in the young Black minds being honed at Historically Black Colleges and Universities or changes in federal sentencing laws?[17] There is a myriad of facts we can highlight to find hope. The downside is it makes certain narratives less provocative. In this way, this cynical worldview accepts and rejects reality. It accepts the idea that things are unchangeable but can only do so by denying the collective value of achievements in our community.

Our oppression didn't end in 1865, but over time our situation has improved substantively. While Confederates didn't walk away quietly and other forms of oppression surely emerged, our quality of life has greatly increased from Emancipation and Jim Crow to now. Without question, our range of self-determination has expanded, even if not in one steady upward line on a graph. This was clear in the list of Black governors, congressmen, mayors, judges, prosecutors, and sheriffs nationwide. To the cynic, that was unimaginable during slavery, but now there are entire large city governments run primarily by African Americans who control the procurement processes and the courthouses. Moreover, Black spending power has reached over a trillion dollars.[18] These are major, longstanding wins, even if they don't result in absolute control over the entire system. The reality of police brutality and Black poverty must still be confronted, but that does not negate these clear signs of progress.

Granted, too many serious racial disparities persist, but to deny Black America's progress since slavery and Jim Crow is intellectually dishonest. It demonstrates a commitment to a cynical ideology that has so demonized every sinew of White America that it can't fathom redemption or explain the reality of any progress. Willie Faye and Mahalia's generation didn't believe White America was irredeemable and neither should we.[19] Redemption may be unlikely for some, but it's not beyond what God can accomplish. That's a choice we make—to embrace moral imagination or cynicism.

Moral imagination is more judicious and accurate than cynicism because cynicism hides what's possible. For instance, medical schools have seen a significant increase in Black students.[20] Under the cynical view, we should've never expected that to happen if it hadn't happened before. Moral imagination leaves the possibility for this kind of achievement open, encouraging one to strive for what they haven't seen or experienced. Cynicism, on the other hand, causes us to have unnecessarily low expectations of ourselves and others. We might never see perfect equality, but improvement is possible. Moral imagination inspires us to strive toward the seemingly improbable but achievable, while cynicism assumes defeat and sets our sights on lesser goals. How many times would Black people have missed great possibilities by restricting ourselves to what was predictable?

Years after Bell and Coates weighed in, from this root, cynicism has become a sort of aesthetic in some academic and activist circles. To be hopeful is a fashion faux pas—a naive mistake in disposition that renders one out of style. Despair is an ornament to be placed prominently on our public witness like a septal nose ring. This has caused some to fetishize oppression. A certain status is given to those who have the most intersectional points of marginalization. Ironically, reveling in your marginalization is actually a display of privilege. Only those with certain advantages have time to be performative about real struggle.

There's nothing cute about donning our oppression like chic ethnic garb. Accepting the limits imposed by racism is counter to the Black Church ethic, which has proof of concept. Our moral imagination gave us the ability to reject those fraudulent boundaries. The late historian Albert J. Raboteau explains in the introduction of a book of slave narratives, "This testimony of the faith of an oppressed people, who, despite their oppression, adapted from the religious resources available to them a ritual of metanoia that made it possible for them not only to deny the brutal limits of slavery but to transcend them."[21]

Pastor and civil rights advocate Fred Shuttlesworth once said, "I had always been a person who believed what God said in the Bible had to come [to pass]."[22] He was describing the role the authority of Scripture played in his activism and overall attitude toward life in the Jim Crow South. The Bible, God's self-revelation, described God as a caring Father and deliverer, and Shuttlesworth not only believed it, but he also acted on that belief in perilous circumstances. It also caused him to believe justice was God's work and as a disciple of Jesus, he was called to that work even if it entailed great suffering.[23]

Moral imagination is faith applied to what we see as possible in our daily lives and it should shape our public witness. It should be the frame through which we evaluate the circumstances and pursue solutions. It's how we know wicked systems can be overcome, anyone can be forgiven and redeemed, and biblical truth is still truth even when Christians have botched the church's public relations. It's the opposite of leaning on our own understanding and cynicism. In dire circumstances, cynicism is death, but moral imagination is life and the meaning therein. It isn't dependent on human forecasts or capabilities. It surpasses conventional wisdom and our reasonable expectations without turning the world into a self-serving fiction. It compels us to pursue what ought to be rather than settling for what's probable based on material measures.

Second Corinthians 4:16-18 provides a basis for the concept of moral imagination:

> We do not lose heart. Though outwardly we are wasting away, yet inwardly we are being renewed day by day. For our light and momentary troubles are achieving for us an eternal glory that far outweighs them all. So we fix our eyes not on what is seen, but on what is unseen, since what is seen is temporary, but what is unseen is eternal.

Furthermore, the psalmist says, "I remain confident of this: I will see the goodness of the Lord in the land of the living" (Psalm 27:13). That should be reflected in our public witness—in how we engage our neighbors, allies, and opposition.

Son of an enslaved mother, the legendary minister Frances J. Grimke approached American racism with a moral imagination not untethered from reality. Theology professor and author Dr. Drew Martin explained,

> Any kind of pessimism he had did not prevent him from acknowledging the benefits of looking on "the bright side." But

> he also pointed to a source of hope and reason to keep fighting that was even stronger. His source of hope was not first and foremost the glimpses of social progress, but rather, "the certainty of the fact that God is on the throne, that right is bound ultimately to triumph, that the spirit of Jesus Christ is in the world" . . . Grimke pressed on not because he believed that social improvement is imminent, but because God is ultimate. On the other hand, he saw no reason for naive optimism, for premature declarations of the end of racism or of other moral evils, or for simplistic statements about the gospel being the only answer needed for social ills in the present age.[24]

Moral imagination is about what we believe is possible and where we derive that notion. It's hope amid oppression, division, and vitriol. It's not a pipe dream. It's the Hebrew vision of the land promised but yet to come. It's what convinced Frederick Douglass to learn to read and write while still in chains and when nothing in his physical line of sight indicated that he'd ever be able to put his talents to use.[25]

Every generation has blind spots and it takes moral imagination to see what the moment is hiding from you. It reveals what's there, but undetected by conventional wisdom. Moral imagination prevents us from being enslaved by the moment. It takes moral imagination to see that conservatism and progressivism aren't the only two approaches to culture and politics and to transcend the culture-war framework altogether. It also forces us to recall that everyone has a story and a testimony even when their anger or prejudices hide it.

It took faith for Willie Faye and Mahalia's generation to believe that conducting themselves with civility and kindness instead of deceit and violence would be worth it. Moral imagination tells us that intellectual honesty and love of neighbor pay off even when the circumstances seem to indicate that lying, contempt, and the dark arts are expedient. It allows us to take a more immediate loss to glorify God and righteously seek a greater good long term.

MORAL IMAGINATION AND GOD'S INSTRUCTION

Those who care deeply about social justice must also see why our actions and attitudes in relation to holiness and righteousness are also necessary for healthy and productive lives in the here and now. If we fight for just systems in society but do our spouse and children the injustice of sexual infidelity, then perhaps we don't truly understand the concepts of justice and righteousness.

Nannie Helen Burroughs implored the church not only to fight for social justice, but also to teach against permissive and pleasure-seeking behavior because it led to spiritual and societal disorder. She admonished those who "neglect[ed] their children, husbands, and wives . . . and could not resist the temptation to join, straight out, sinners in dens [and] brothels."[26] She asked "what is our brand of Christianity and what is the Church for" if we couldn't be moved to tackle human degeneracy.[27]

In 1892, abolitionist, suffragist, and poet Frances Harper lamented how debasement and sin sends into "our streets women whose laughter is sadder than their tears."[28] She urged parents to guide both their sons and daughters away from growing up to be "children of pleasure" instead of living lives of self-control and self-respect. Both Black Christian women understood that while we seem to be enjoying socially liberated lives, it takes wisdom and moral imagination to see the consequences of debauchery before they've vested.

Moral imagination isn't just about believing God can use us to change society or acknowledging our opponent's humanity when hidden behind insults and hateful behavior. It's also about following God's instructions when the benefits of obedience aren't clear and when it conflicts with our desires and self-perception. When hormones are rushing through our body, it reminds us that a moment of pleasure can lead to a lifetime of pain and sorrow. Getting what we want in the moment isn't always good.

Furthermore, moral imagination prevents us from creating golden calves when God's ways don't match how our finite minds conceive the world and our desired outcomes. It involves promoting what God says is moral even when it's counterintuitive or unpleasant. It's having faith in God's design, believing that how he says things should work will lead to flourishing even when popular culture vehemently disagrees. We must remember that God's instructions don't have to meet humanity's approval. We must meet his approval. This is a very difficult concept in a culture that makes the individual and its feelings the center of the universe. Moral imagination emboldens us to uphold timeless Christian convictions even when popular culture mocks and threatens. It reveals that there's love in inconvenient truths.

The Black Church tradition has always found solace in the exodus narrative. We intimately identify with the enslaved Hebrews who God used Moses to deliver. That biblical motif was meaningful and proved God is in the business of liberation, but Exodus doesn't end there. God didn't deliver them so they'd have license to live however they saw fit (Exodus 21–24). Freedom from the hands of Pharaoh didn't mean the Hebrews were righteous or prepared to enter the promised land. God still had to give them the law to reveal his nature, wisdom, and standards for righteousness and justice (Exodus 34:6-7; Leviticus 11:45). He still had to give them direction and instruction or their freedom would have very little value.

Without guidance, they'd be delivered from the sin of slavery into the slavery of sin.[29] Again, to be free without direction or moral compass is to be lost. Freedom misconceived and misused always leads to bondage of another kind. We "were called to be free," but we ought not use our "freedom to indulge the flesh" (Galatians 5:13). Freedom is more than untethered self-expression and wildly doing "as thou wilt" in an open space. Some liberation theology scholars tend to skip over the second half of Exodus. They want to take the liberation but leave the moral imperatives required by God, the liberator. Exodus shows us the importance of justice and moral order. God releases the captives and lovingly refuses to leave them to their own devices. The Black Church's social action tradition recognized that seeking to liberate people without truth and obedience is like freeing them into a lion's den.

Reverend Fred Shuttlesworth understood the importance of social justice and moral order. He saw how they were both necessary for human flourishing. He fought against racism in the heart of Jim Crow, courageously putting himself in harm's way. He also pushed against the violent and depraved Juke Joints in his community that took too many men away from their families in sin and in caskets. He knew his people deserved freedom and that their freedom would be curtailed if their own culture led them into violence and destructive behavior. This is true for any community. Moral imagination gives us hope for future justice and gives us reason to hold onto God's standards of holiness.

"To obey is better than sacrifice" (1 Samuel 15:22). Faith involves turning all our thoughts, ideas, and opinions over to God and trusting that his Word is true. Even our concepts of love and justice can be distorted. We must examine them with biblical scrutiny to make sure they conform with what God says is right and compassionate. Otherwise, we might limit love to sentimentality and rob it of discernment. Without moral imagination, social justice can become vengeful rather than redemptive. It transitions from being about treating people with human dignity to promoting every excess of human expression. Moral imagination allows us to see beyond our wants, predispositions, and the predominant storylines of our time.

As slave narratives described, one's conversion to Christianity was understood as a "rebirth"—"being made entirely new"—a "change of heart" and a "radical reorientation of personality," which impacted their daily condition and redefined "their identity and self-worth."[30] Jesus had compassion and grace for those whose identity caused them to be marginalized, but he also gave them full human dignity and the agency (or choice) to seek righteousness themselves.

If we're honest with ourselves, we know our wisdom is limited and our deep intuitions and feelings have led us astray more times than we can count. We're reluctant to admit that when we want things our way, but it's true. A faith that doesn't trust God's Word over the culture and human desires is no faith at all. The sins committed against us don't justify our sins. It takes moral imagination to comprehend that in a grievance-obsessed culture.

In a sincere effort to love our neighbors well and refrain from repeating the bigoted errors of the American church's past, we're tempted to affirm behaviors and systems of belief clearly at odds with the Word of God and his design. The world tells us that to be loving we must reject what the Bible says is true, especially concerning sexual ethics. Some have cleverly described it as "evolving,"[31] but with moral imagination we can be compassionate without turning the truth into clay in the hands of broken humanity. It helps us to understand that hard teaching that might hurt our feelings in the moment can actually rescue us from a life of sin. In a time when many Christians are just repeating talking points from secular influencers, we can't throw our hands up and surrender to popular culture.

The Bible says, “In fact, this is love for God: to keep his commands. And his commands are not burdensome” (1 John 5:3). We can uphold Christian principles and be loving. We don’t need to conflate love and affirmation to protect our neighbors with tenacity and grace.

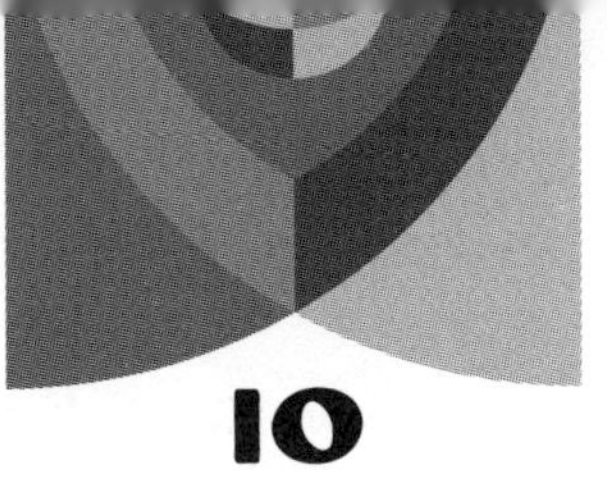

10

GOD DON'T WANT NO COWARD SOLDIER

God don't want no
He don't want no coward soldiers
He don't want no coward soldiers in His band

James Herndon

IN THE BLACK AMERICAN LEXICON, to be called "scary" or "sorry" is a most piercing rebuke. Respectively, they are behavioral characterizations of a person who lacks courage or integrity. To be described as scary means you're unwilling to stand up for yourself, your community, or your convictions. You lack confidence and are acting cowardly to the point of faithlessness. The Bible says, "The wicked flee though no one pursues, but the righteous are as bold as a lion" (Proverbs 28:1). If you're referred to as sorry, it indicates that you were unreliable, shiftless, lacking conviction, or easily bought off. For example, a politician is sorry if she doesn't keep her campaign promises or isn't assertive and shrewd. A worker was sorry if he avoided his tasks or refused to take responsibility for his behavior.

In the book of Amos, Amaziah the priest had a sorry public witness. Instead of challenging unjust and immoral authority like the prophet Amos, he cozied up with the king and tried to expel Amos from the kingdom for speaking the truth to power (Amos 7). He was looking out for himself rather than serving God and protecting the vulnerable self-sacrificially. In a sermon, Dr. William Augustus Jones called him "a slave of the system."[1]

In the public square Christians should be conducting ourselves with compassion, thoughtfulness, and courage. However, in many instances, our public witness can also accurately be characterized as scary and sorry. This manifests itself in a number of ways. If we examine closely enough, we see:

- Christian politicians who lack the integrity to represent racial justice in the Republican Party or to stand for the sanctity of life and religious liberty in the Democratic Party.
- Professional-class Christians who allow their career ambitions to outpace their convictions; those who exploit consumers to move up the corporate ladder or deny unpopular Christian convictions to fit into cocktail party circles.
- Christian professors and students who don't have the fortitude or the apologetic to resist and challenge the dominance of secular progressivism in universities.
- Christian influencers who present themselves as leaders in the church but seek approval from secular entertainers and activists and are unwilling to question even the most extreme aspects of things like gender ideology.
- Christians who think true believers must support their political party and refuse to apply the Bible's love imperative to their neighbors in the LGBT+ community.
- Preachers who won't preach in support of redemptive social justice or the traditional Christian sexual ethic in fear of overly ideological congregants.

Regrettably, I've fit into more than one of those categories in my life. Thankfully, the Christian ethic doesn't give up on those of us who've been scary or sorry. Like Peter after his three denials, it compels us to be redeemed and pursue a better way forward. With prayer and the Holy Spirit, we're all capable of being more like Amos than Amaziah in our public witness. The Black Church social action tradition provides many inspirational examples of how to engage more courageously.

According to theologian G. K. Chesterton, "Courage is almost a contradiction in terms. It means a strong desire to live taking the form of a readiness to die."[2] Faithful engagement won't necessarily call for us to die, but it will force us to face peer pressure and cancel culture boldly. Dr. Martin Luther King Jr. once called Rev. Fred Shuttlesworth "the most courageous civil rights fighter in the South."[3] As discussed earlier, Shuttlesworth was willing to put himself in harm's way to do what was right. He called himself a biblicist and an actionist, meaning he had a devout faith in the authority of Scripture while believing right doctrine compelled the Christian into social action.[4] He courageously defended the gospel and the human dignity of his neighbors. This type of courage is necessary to be ambassadors of Christ in the public square.

As discussed, the combination and consistent application of four traits make the Black Church social action tradition distinctive and particularly instructive in transcending today's culture war mentality: (1) connecting the spiritual and sociopolitical advocacy; (2) upholding social justice and moral order; (3) acknowledging internal sin; and (4) exemplifying moral imagination. In conclusion, I'll summarize each of these points.

CONNECTING THE SPIRITUAL AND SOCIOPOLITICAL ADVOCACY

The culture war has caused many Christians to detach our sociopolitical engagement from our spirituality, or, alternatively, to hide our cultural and ideological preferences behind spiritual language and religious symbolism. This allows us to rationalize behavior that's counter to Christian principles. Otherwise, we wouldn't be able to justify political violence and policies that endanger born and unborn lives. Faith should be directing and inspiring our actions in the public square. Instead, we're led by acts of the flesh. Christian civic engagement is riddled with hatred, dissension, factions, and idolatry. We've been lured into opposition-centered politics, which means we're primarily motivated by rivalries and vengeance. We want to prove our opponents wrong and see their humiliation more than we want to do what's right because we're following self-interest and contempt.

The Bible says, "Walk by the Spirit, and you will not gratify the desires of the flesh. For the flesh desires what is contrary to the Spirit" (Galatians 5:16-17). The Black Church social action tradition modeled how to apply the fruit of the Spirit—love, peace, forbearance, self-control, etc.—because it didn't separate spiritual life from advocacy. According to her obituary in the *New York Times*, Mahalia was "convinced that everything she said or did rested on the word of God."[5] This meant God's Word set the standard and the terms of engagement—not their appetites, their opponents' tactics, or the circumstances. Their social action was genuinely inspired by the authority of Scripture and its promises. The gospel was more than just a call to action; it was a call to salvation, holiness, and truth.

We see this connection in the life and work of Frances Harper, whose public witness was expressed through art and advocacy. Almost all of her poems and speeches cited the Bible. She treated the Bible as the authority, not a source secondary to ideological commitments. According to Harper, humanity is saved by faith and "the law of liberty is the law of God, and is antecedent to all human legislation."[6] She masterfully condemned those who used the Bible to defend slavery in verse:

An infidel could do no more
To hide his country's guilty blot,

Than spread God's Holy record o'er
The loathsome leprous spot.[7]

In her famous speech "We Are All Bound Together," she explained how the oppression of Black people "crippled the moral strength and paralyzed the spiritual energies of the white men in the country."[8] She knew our public witness and our spiritual state were inextricably tied together. With her words and her social action, she fought against immorality and injustice. She warned about how debauchery "traced a path to shame and woe" and was also on the ground advocating for abolition, equal rights, and education for African American women.[9]

Like Frances Harper, if Christians are going to speak into the culture war with vision and moral imagination, our sociopolitical engagement we must be led by the fruit of the Spirit. We cannot stigmatize entire races and classes of people, calling them by slurs like "libtards," "welfare queen," or "Karen." Our standards aren't dictated by the circumstances or the tactics of our sneering opponents. They're dictated by our spiritual walk.

SOCIAL JUSTICE AND MORAL ORDER

Dr. Mildred Fay Jefferson, the child of a schoolteacher and a pastor, "was the first African American woman to graduate from Harvard Medical School in 1951" and the first female surgeon to work at Boston University's Medical Center.[10] Due to racism, she had to wait twenty-one years before the American Board of Surgery would certify her as a surgeon.[11] As a Black Methodist woman, Jefferson said her faith inspired her to become a physician and a pro-life advocate.[12]

> I became a physician in order to help save lives . . . I will not accept the proposition that the doctor should relinquish the role of healer to become the executioner.

> The Hippocratic tradition fused with the Judeo-Christian sanctity of life ethic requires that a doctor demand of oneself a high standard of moral conduct.[13]

She would join forces with Dolores B. Grier, another Black Christian advocate who was raised in the Baptist Church, later converting to Catholicism while living in Harlem. Grier was convinced to join the movement against abortion by Rev. Jesse Jackson and believed the push for abortion in Black communities was a product of racism.[14]

> We do believe that more than anything else, abortion is racism. It is a way of pruning the Black population. . . . Black women never demonstrated, demanded, or even requested the right to an abortion. We've been asking for the right to decent housing, the right to education, the right to healthcare, and all we've been given, free of charge, is the right to kill our unborn child.[15]

Both Jefferson and Grier saw the interconnection between justice and moral order. Based on their Christian convictions and a thorough analysis of the issue, they concluded that abortion was unjust, immoral—and therefore, had to be opposed. This was a matter of divine command, not a subject in which one's opinion could be outsourced to an ideological tribe (Proverbs. 6:16-17).

This ideologically heterodox point of view was a hallmark of Willie Faye and Mahalia's generation. They understood the need for social justice and moral order, and they proved secular progressivism isn't a prerequisite for genuine social justice engagement. In fact, the history of Black Christians dismantles two of the primary misconceptions coming from the ideological Right and Left respectively: (1) white conservative Christianity is the purest and normative form of the faith; (2) progressivism is synonymous with compassion, intelligence, and relevance.

First, Christianity was in Africa decades before it arrived in Western Europe, and the African Church fathers like Tertullian, Athanasius, Augustine, and Origen fought for Christian orthodoxy amid an onslaught of heresies. Furthermore, as Dr. Esau McCaulley explains in his book *Reading While Black*, the Black Church's social action tradition centered on Christ and the authority of Scripture. It was a living model of orthodoxy (right doctrine) and orthopraxy (right actions), unlike many conservative and progressive Christians today who either focus on piety *or* social action.

Second, as Dr. William Augustus Jones noted, "The Black Church is the only institution in the Black community with historic continuity."[16] The primary stream of the Black Church tradition saw truth, sin, and freedom much differently than secular progressives. The commentary of Nannie Helen Burrows asserted that love wasn't simply the affirmation of another's self-perception or lifestyle, but rather self-sacrifice. It was caring and devoted, but could also render a candid critique that stings. Dr. Gardner C. Taylor explained that academic knowledge was good, but insufficient without moral knowledge and wisdom. He warned us about intellectual trends that overlook the consequences of sinful self-indulgence. He knew we couldn't socially construct our way around the results of loose living.

The civil rights movement was primarily a Christian movement and no American movement has been more relevant. Its relevance didn't come through conforming to the world or seeking the validation of secular activists and academics or any political party. It was relevant because it responded to the issues of its day with boldness and innovation while standing on timeless truth.

The Black Church social action tradition can't be placed in a progressive or conservative ideological box. Its theology makes it philosophically ambidextrous, meaning it can seek societal progress while preserving certain timeless values. Although it was far from perfect, they understood broken systems and institutions needed to change, but the biblical conception of truth and sin did not and could not. Nannie Helen Burroughs once said Christian principles "are the same yesterday, today and forever. There is no substitute for them. They are divine."[17]

The culture war has created morality Christians on one side and social justice Christians on the other. We've been lured into choosing one of these two flawed sides and completely disavowing the other. That shouldn't be the case. Like the Christian leaders in this book, we must represent the whole counsel of God in the public square, not only the principles our side allows us to support. We shouldn't compromise the integrity of our public witness by merely becoming agents of conservativism or progressivism.

The Christian public witness is about courageously choosing the right position on issues rather than just choosing a side and simplemindedly accepting its entire agenda. If party A is right on three out of four issues, then we might have good reason to more generally support them over party B. However, we must be vocal about our disagreement with party A on that fourth issue and oppose them on it in no uncertain terms. For example, Christian Democrats should vocally support religious liberty and stand against inappropriate parts of the Left's sexual education curricula. Christian Republicans should support humane treatment of immigrants and pressure their party to develop a serious healthcare plan.

THE SIN IN ME AND THE REDEEMABILITY OF THEM

The culture war also indulges the human tendency to overestimate our rightness and righteousness. Like the praying Pharisee, we exalt ourselves and condemn others in culture and politics (Luke 18:9-14). We pretend our side is all good and our opposition is completely evil, but that proposition conveniently flattens reality. Our side might be right on some very important issues and the other side might be dead wrong on a number of accounts, but our self-righteousness is unwarranted. We too are fallen, our motives are often mixed, and even when we're pursuing a good cause, we can fall prey to a tyrannical or malicious spirit. Neither the most vicious racist nor the most zealous abortionist is beyond redemption. We must oppose their unrighteousness without contempt or vengeance. We need to replace the good vs. evil framework with a worldview that recognizes the image of God in others and the sin in us. We have to be able to tell others when they're wrong without also saying they're worthless and have no contribution to make to society.

Furthermore, our wrongs aren't justified even if our opponent has been more wrong. Morality by comparison seeks self-justification by finding a worse error on the other side, but if your favorite politician lies ten times and a politician on the other party lies twenty times, your politician is not absolved. When we refuse to hold our side accountable, we not only lose credibility in the public square, but we are committing the sin of partiality. That's unjust.

With grace and tenacity Willie Faye and Mahalia's generation resisted the urge to become evil to fight evil. Founding member of SNCC Diane Nash was arrested in 1960 for sit-ins. She said there was no English word to describe what powered the civil rights movement. They best described it with the Greek term *agapē*, which is an unconditional and self-sacrificial love for all people, even those who oppressed you. According to Nash, the first principle of agape love was "people are never your enemy . . . Unjust political and economic systems are enemies."[18] She went on to recount a story about a White restaurant manager in Nashville who was initially against desegregation but eventually became an ally, working to persuade other White businessmen to desegregate. In the spirit of the movement, she then queried, "Wouldn't it have been a shame if we had killed or injured him, thinking that he was the enemy? It was not the person who was the enemy. It was his racism."[19]

The patron saint of self-examination Nannie Helen Burroughs would also remind us that the enemy isn't just in others, it's inside of us as well. Burroughs was well aware of the real impact of racism, yet she insisted that even an oppressed people have responsibility to improve themselves morally. She had the moral knowledge to understand that in the midst of fighting injustice, we must prayerfully inspect ourselves for sin. She courageously addressed the errors in White America without pretending that her own people were without shortcomings of their own making. She urged her people to "raise the standard" and seek "uprightness of character and loftiness of purpose."

In the book of Judges, Gideon was commissioned by God to liberate his people from the cruel hand of the Midianites who were systematically persecuting the Israelites—burning their houses and fields, stealing their crops and livestock, and leaving them impoverished and terrified. Gideon would have to deal with the Midianites to free his people who were so afraid that they were living in caves. But first, God told him to tear down his father's altar of Baal and all the attendant idols in the town (Judges 6:25-26). Apparently, his father was the custodian of the town's Baal-sanctuary.[20] The idolatry was close to home. Consequently, before his people could be delivered from external oppression, they had some internal issues that needed to be addressed.

Tearing down the altar of Baal would be an attack on the local establishment and would certainly arouse anger in his community. Nonetheless, Gideon had to first knock down the idols his people worshiped to help deliver them from the bondage of their own making and from the bondage of the Midianites. It's time for

Christians who lean right and left to tear down the altars to the ideological idols that promote injustice and immorality in our own culture. We must be courageous enough to face the ire of those on our side when it's necessary to obey God and be the light in our community's blind spots. For too long, the culture war has lured us into focusing on either social justice or moral order. That's created an incomplete public witness that condones things God has clearly required us to combat.

We must first be humble about our own sin nature and the need for self-examination. The influencers in our culture will give us an alibi for our every failure. If you fail a class because you didn't study, someone will be there to tell you the professor was biased. Our politicians will pander to us, and for an audience, bloggers will try to manipulate us through flattery or identity idolatry. But our race, sex, and class have nothing to do with our character or competence. We know all our issues aren't someone else's fault. As hard as it is, we must reject narratives that justify our wrongdoing or make it seem like everything is our opponent's fault. Transparency and admissions of guilt are prohibited in the culture war, but our public confessions glorify God. When we're honest about what we've done wrong, we also gain credibility with outsiders and we can better pursue civil pluralism, democracy, and more importantly true neighborliness.

Christians must also seek to understand the other side's true objectives, fears, and pain. Conservative Christian should care about their LGBT+ neighbors and be willing to advocate for their basic civil liberties. They shouldn't condemn them by saying, "You should be more like me." They should lift them up and say, "I'm fallen too. Let us both take our brokenness to the cross and venture to be more like Christ." Progressive Christians have to care about the conservative White males who are dying from deaths of despair—overdoses and suicides—at alarming rates.[21]

Not only do they have to care, but they have to be willing to advocate for them, even if they wouldn't return the favor. This doesn't mean all their positions are right, but Christian must care about their struggles.

We seek near absolute power for one side, but the truth is none of us are fit to steward it. We need to listen and learn from other groups. As I read the Bible, I see no indication that God's own people ever had all the answers or had a monopoly on good ideas and good works. They were often blessed by the insights and compassion of outsiders and sickened by the fruit of their own understanding (Luke 10:25-37; Joshua 2; Exodus 32). God gave us the Word, but he didn't give any one group all the answers. We're broken. Our intellect is incomplete and can lead to destruction. Even our concept of love can be distorted—love for our own has often been treated as the justification for wickedness toward others. Conservatism opposed abolition and the civil rights movement. Progressivism ushered in eugenics. Conservatism has yet to present us with a perfect meritocracy. Progressivism has yet to prove that replacing God with autonomy can create a perfect utopia. Neither has proof of concept and we all have plenty of reasons to be humble as we address others.

Every conservative is not malicious, and every progressive isn't intellectually dishonest. Christians should be able to list several things their side of the ideological spectrum gets wrong. They should also be able to name some of the virtues on the other side. If we can't do that then we've been indoctrinated. We have to get past the caricatures and misrepresentations to ascertain the good they're trying to achieve, even if we disagree with their conclusion, which is why it's important for us to be honest about the faults of the Black Church's social action tradition too. Historically, it suffered from sexism, classism, and was often less than Christlike toward same-sex attracted churchgoers. We can't correct those things if we're too prideful to acknowledge them.

What if we all refused to see our sociopolitical opposition as enemies or as purely evil? What if we battled them through debate, legislation, and protest without contempt and critiqued ourselves? Willie Faye and Mahalia's generation proves it wouldn't make us less effective, but it would certainly make us more faithful. If the church were to adopt this posture, the culture-war mentality would shrivel up and die.

MORAL IMAGINATION

The Black Church social action tradition was a negro spiritual in action. It courageously refused to be arrested by fear or despair. That was the key to maintaining a deep abiding joy through slavery, the end of Reconstruction, and Jim Crow. Mahalia's description of the difference between gospel music and the blues, captures the spirit and moral imagination of the tradition: "Blues are the songs of despair. Gospel songs are the songs of hope. When you sing gospel you have the feeling there is a cure for what's wrong, but when you are through with the blues, you've got nothing to rest on."[22]

Her explanation also describes the difference in spirit between Willie Faye and Mahalia's generation and some of today's social justice efforts. Willie Faye told me I could achieve anything if I worked hard. All her children and grandchildren knew she expected us to succeed, and although racism was a real hurdle, it wouldn't be an acceptable excuse. Some social justice advocates today say high expectations for certain children are harmful because the system will hold them down.[23] While we do need to keep fighting unjust systems, low expectations smother their agency—the reality that their efforts and decisions matter. Moral imagination maintains room for the possible while fighting for more justice and equality in the moment. Pessimism settles for rage or antagonism and forecloses what's unseen and unlikely. It's a faithless way of protecting ourselves from disappointment.

In her poem "The Present Age," Frances Harper implored Christians to spend their time aspiring to improve their era rather than complaining about it as if we had no say in the matter. It's a literary call to transcend cynicism and defeatism. Instead of seeing ourselves as victims of circumstance, she encourages us to imagine what could and should be and get to work.

To side with justice, truth and right
And act a noble part.
To save from ignorance and vice
The poorest and humblest child
To make our age the fairest one
On which the sun has smiled;
To plant roots of coming years
In mercy, love and truth;
And bid our weary, saddened earth
Again renew her youth.
Oh! earnest hearts! toil on in hope,
'Till darkness shrinks from light . . .
Blame not the age, nor think it full
Of evil and unrest;
But say of every age,
"This one shall be the best."

God has given his people purpose and influence in the present age. We're not merely spectators. We don't just sit and observe the outcome like some kind of lottery. We have agency and we have a God who cares and listens. We have a God who will change the course of human history for us and through us. Neither racial injustice nor cancel culture is invincible. They will be defeated. While we can't know exactly when, inasmuch as it's up to us, we'll work for them to end "soon and very soon." We must work as if we know the victory is forthcoming and know that our every sacrifice on the way glorifies God.

We all feel embattled. Progressives worry about attacks on democracy and diversity programs, and conservatives worry about attacks on the family ethic. No matter how high the stakes are during an election or in regard to a cultural issue, we can never be enslaved by the moment. The circumstances don't dictate our standards or our spiritual disposition.

A PATH FORWARD FOR THE WHOLE CHURCH

Two of Mahalia Jackson's most classic gospel renditions were her recordings of "Amazing Grace" and "His Eye Is on the Sparrow." While many of the hymns she sang were written by Black writers, "Amazing Grace," which became an anthem among her enslaved ancestors, was a poem written by John Newton in 1772.[24] Newton was an Englishman and reformed slave trader.[25] "His Eye Is on the Sparrow" was written by Civilla Durfee Martin, a White Canadian American woman in 1906.[26] Mahalia took those compositions and sang them in ways the original writers could've never imagined. In a real way, her awe-inspiring renditions of these songs were collaborations with Christians from different times, lands, and ethnic backgrounds. They'd never meet on earth, but God would use all of them to inspire countless people who were also worlds and decades apart.

Thankfully, Newton's work didn't just belong to Englishmen and Martin's work didn't merely belong to Canadian Americans. They belonged to the universal church. Similarly, while the work of the Black Church social action tradition should be celebrated and bring a sense of godly pride to Black Christians, it belongs to the church as a whole. Willie Faye and Mahalia's generation applied a universal ethic that all of us can strive toward. It's a framework that all Bible-believing denominations, every class, and every race can embrace and build upon. That tradition best serves as a significant piece to a greater and more collaborative kingdom work.

When Black preachers reference Chinese evangelist Shi Meiyu in an illustration, quote the English pastor Charles H. Spurgeon, or cite Peruvian theologian Gustavo Gutierrez, they're not misappropriating another culture. They're tapping into a resource that all of Christianity can claim as its own. These resources might have been revealed first in a different culture, but inasmuch as they're biblical, they came from the same source.

Dr. Martin Luther King Jr. was named after the German monk Martin Luther. Martin Luther, the father of Protestantism, said Saint Augustine, an African theologian, was the greatest influence on theology after the Bible.[27] The best of our theologies and faithful efforts are deeply connected because they're fruit of the same gospel root. Our greatest work will come from us resourcing the best of all Christian efforts throughout history. This book isn't made to exalt the Black Church, but to add to the annals of the body to inspire unity and engagement that values moral order and social justice.

We are not the source. At our best, God is working through us. The work of the Black Church social action tradition would've been filthy rags without God's Spirit and providence (Isaiah 64:6). If our work is righteous, it can only be credited to God. God used the apostle Paul, a persecutor of the church, to help build and instruct the church. He used a former slave trader to create a beautiful hymn about human brokenness and he used faithful but imperfect people in Willie Faye and Mahalia's generation to model a beautiful approach to civic engagement. That means, despite our brokenness, he can use believers from all backgrounds today to create another beautiful rendition of Christian social engagement that transcends the conservative-versus-progressive paradigm. And this time we must do it together.

On issues like family-oriented policy and racial justice, let us not limit ourselves to the confines of the ideological Left or Right or stay in our partisan silos. Instead, we should innovatively merge the best insights and attributes from all parts of the Bible-believing church throughout the centuries and develop a public witness that stands on truth and sacrifices for neighbor in love.

ACKNOWLEDGMENTS

TO GOD BE THE GLORY! This book wouldn't have been possible without my beautiful wife and best friend, Sumhr. You held me down throughout this process and picked up the slack when it became far more challenging than I anticipated. I'm a better person because of you, and I've received your patience and grace in a far bigger portion than I deserve. Thank you to my parents, Ronald and Susan Giboney for always being in my corner and all your sacrifices. To my sons—Cooper, Chase, Crue—thank you for inspiring me. Thank you to my uncles, Bishop Thomas P. Cooper and Councilman Dennis Cooper for the depth of family history.

Major shout-out to my friends who served as sounding boards for this book. I greatly appreciate Dr. Esau McCaulley, Lisa Fields, Dr. Charlie Dates, Steven Harris, Sho Baraka, and Dr. CJ Rhodes for their feedback. Thanks to my agent, attorney, and friend Donovan D. Potter Sr. Thank you to the editors and staff at InterVarsity Press.

Lastly, thank you to Willie Faye and Mahalia's generation for their sacrifices and the legacy they left. I pray I did it justice.

Willie Faye Cooper and her grandson Justin Giboney in 1982.

NOTES

DEDICATION

[1]Horace Livingston, "Coopers Celebrate 30th Wedding Anniversary," *The Voice*, Thursday, July 12, 1979.

INTRODUCTION

[1]Philip Dray, *Capitol Men: The Epic Story of Reconstruction Through the Lives of the First Black Congressmen* (Boston: Mariner Books, 2008), 40-45, 238.

[2]Dray, *Capitol Men*, 40-41.

[3]Library of Congress, *Missionary Record*, July 5, 1873, accessed December 2024, https://chroniclingamerica.loc.gov/lccn/sn83025781/.

[4]Dray, *Capitol Men*, 40-51.

[5]N. Louise Bailey, Mary L. Morgan, and Carolyn R. Taylor, eds., *Biographical Directory of the South Carolina Senate, 1776–1985*, 3 vols. (Columbia: University of South Carolina Press, 1986); Bernard E. Powers, "Richard Harvey Cain," *South Carolina Encyclopedia* (Columbia: University of South Carolina, Institute for Southern Studies, 2016), www.scencyclopedia.org/sce/entries/cain-richard-harvey/.

[6]Dray, *Capitol Men*, 172-176.

[7]Richard H. Cain, "A Nation of Croakers," January, 1874, speech in Congress on the Civil Rights Bill, accessed March 10, 2025, https://loa-shared.s3.amazonaws.com/static/pdf/Cain_Croakers.pdf.

[8]Cain, "A Nation of Croakers."

[9]Dray, *Capitol Men*, 45.

[10]Dray, *Capitol Men*, 1.

[11]Justin E. Giboney, "Backbone, Mouthpiece, and Good News," *Comment*, December 7, 2023, https://comment.org/backbone-mouthpiece-and-good-news/.

[12]Dray, *Capitol Men*, 45.

[13]Dray, *Capitol Men*, 45.

[14]Giboney, "Backbone, Mouthpiece, and Good News."

[15]*Mahalia Jackson: The Glory & the Power*, directed by Jeff Scheftel, narrated by Paul Winfield (Xenon, 1997), DVD.

1. IT'S TIME TO MAKE A CHANGE

[1]David G. Sansing, "Martin Sennet Conner," *Mississippi Encyclopedia*, July 10, 2017, https://mississippiencyclopedia.org/entries/martin-sennet-conner/.

[2]Leah Willingham, "Black Man's Death in Mississippi: Lynching or Suicide?" AP News, May 23, 2021, https://apnews.com/article/us-news-mississippi-racial-injustice-suicides-race-and-ethnicity-6f78ac5838974164c50d4991a2b0efba; Julius E. Thompson, "The Great Depression, 1930–1939," in *Lynchings in Mississippi: A History, 1865–1965* (Jefferson, NC: McFarland & Company, 2011).

[3]"The Great Migration (1910–1970)," National Archives, accessed December 16, 2024, www.archives.gov/research/african-americans/migrations/great-migration#:~:text=The%20First%20Great%20Migration%20(1910,leaving%20their%20industrial%20jobs%20vacant.

[4]May Beth Swetnam Mathews, *Doctrine and Race: African American Evangelicals and Fundamentalism Between the Wars* (Tuscaloosa, AL: University of Alabama Press, 2017), 133.

[5]Lonnie Bunch, "Mahalia Jackson: Gospel Takes Flight," National Museum of African American History & Culture, accessed December 16, 2024, https://nmaahc.si.edu/explore/stories/mahalia-jackson-gospel-takes-flight.

[6]Laurraine Goreau, *Just Mahalia, Baby* (Gretna, LA: Pelican Publishing Company, 1975), 4, 14; Bunch, "Mahalia Jackson: Gospel Takes Flight."

[7]Goreau, *Just Mahalia, Baby*, 21, 27.

[8]Goreau, *Just Mahalia, Baby*, 23

[9]*Mahalia Jackson: The Glory & the Power*, directed by Jeff Scheftel, narrated by Paul Winfield (Xenon, 1997), DVD.

[10]Goreau, *Just Mahalia, Baby*, 27, 35, 45, 47.

[11]Goreau, *Just Mahalia, Baby*, 40, 41, 50; *Mahalia Jackson: The Glory & the Power*.

[12]*Mahalia Jackson: The Glory & the Power*.

[13]*Mahalia Jackson: The Glory & the Power*.

[14]Goreau, *Just Mahalia, Baby*, 11, 13.

[15]Equal Justice Initiative, "Lynching in America: Confronting a Legacy of Racial Terror," February 2015, 8, https://time.com/wp-content/uploads/2015/02/eji_lynching_in_america_summary.pdf.

[16]Equal Justice Initiative, "Lynching in America," 10.

[17]Equal Justice Initiative, "Lynching in America."

[18]Michael Murphy, "The Troubling Past of Forced Sterilization of Black Woman and Girls in Mississippi and the South," *Mississippi Free Press*, June 4, 2021, www.mississippifreepress.org/the-troubling-past-of-forced-sterilization-of-black-women-and-girls-in-mississippi-and-the-south/; Linda Villarosa, "The Long Shadow of Eugenics in America," *New York Times*, June 8, 2022, www.nytimes.com/2022/06/08/magazine/eugenics-movement-america.html.

[19]Horace Boyer, *How Sweet the Sound: The Golden Age of Gospel* (Washington, DC: Elliot & Clark Publishing, 1995), 85.

[20]Esau McCaulley, *Reading While Black: African American Biblical Interpretation as an Exercise in Hope* (Downers Grove, IL: InterVarsity Press, 2020), 5-8.

[21]Jonathan Eig, *King: A Life* (New York: Farrar, Straus and Giroux, 2023), 434.

[22]Eric C. Lincoln and Lawrence Mamiya, *The Black Church in the African American Experience* (Durham, NC: Duke University Press, 1990), 197.

[23]Mathews, *Doctrine and Race*, 141.

[24]Hiram R. Revels, "(1871) Revels Urges Desegregation of District of Columbia School," senatorial address in the United States Senate, January 28, 2007, www.blackpast.org/african-american-history/1871-senator-hiram-revels-calls-end-segregated-schools.

[25]Frederick Douglass, "Frederick Douglass Declares There Is 'No Progress Without Struggle,'" SHEC: Resources for Teachers, accessed December 16, 2024, https://shec.ashp.cuny.edu/items/show/1245.

[26]Eig, *King: A Life*, 38.

[27]"History of PNBC," PNBC.org, accessed March 10, 2025, https://pnbc.org/content/history-of-the-pnbc/.

[28]The Martin Luther King Jr. Research and Education Institute, "Progressive National Baptist Convention (PNBC)," November 14, 1961, https://kinginstitute.stanford.edu/progressive-national-baptist-convention-pnbc; "History of PNBC."

[29]Mary R. Sawyer, *Black Ecumenism: Implementing the Demands of Justice* (Valley Forge: Trinity Press International, 1994), 35.

[30]*Mahalia Jackson: The Glory & the Power.*

[31]Goreau, *Just Mahalia, Baby*, 60.

[32]Boyer, *How Sweet the Sound*, 30, 42.

[33]*Mahalia Jackson: The Glory & the Power.*

[34]Taylor Branch, *Parting the Waters: America in the King Years 1954–65* (New York: Simon & Schuster Paperbacks, 1988), 882.

[35]Boyer, *How Sweet the Sound*, 10.

[36]Kay Mills, *This Little Light of Mine* (Lexington: University Press of Kentucky, 2007), 17, 60, 77.

[37]Albert Raboteau, *Slave Religion: The Invisible Institution in the Antebellum South* (Oxford: Oxford University Press, 2004), 212-13; E. Franklin Frazier and C. Eric Lincoln, *The Negro Church in America* (New York: Schocken Books, 1974), 23.

[38]Lincoln and Mamiya, *The Black Church*, 200-201.

[39]Raboteau, *Slave Religion*, 213.

[40]Lincoln and Mamiya, *The Black Church*, 195; Vince Bantu, *Gospel Haymanot: A Constructive Theology and Critical Reflection on African and Diasporic Christianity* (Chicago: Urban Ministries, Inc., 2020), 7-42.

[41]Bantu, *Gospel Haymanot*, 7.

[42]Raboteau, *Slave Religion*, 213.

[43]Lincoln and Mamiya, *The Black Church*, 201.

[44]Lincoln and Mamiya, *The Black Church*, 200.

[45]"Born in Slavery: Slave Narratives from the Federal Writers' Project, 1936 to 1938," WPA Slave Narrative Project (North Carolina Narratives, Vol. 2, Part 1), Federal Writers' Project, U.S. Work Projects Administration (USWPA), in Library of Congress, Digital Collections, accessed December 16, 2024, www.loc.gov/collections/slave-narratives-from-the-federal-writers-project-1936-to-1938.

[46]Bantu, *Gospel Haymanot*, 8, 43.

[47]Lincoln and Mamiya, *The Black Church*, 92.

[48]Frazier and Lincoln, *The Negro Church in America*, 35-50.

[49]Frazier and Lincoln, *The Negro Church in America*, 47.

[50]Studs Terkel, "Mahalia Jackson Find Her Way," *DownBeat*, December 11, 1958.

[51]Frazier and Lincoln, *The Negro Church in America*, 165.

[52]Frazier and Lincoln, *The Negro Church in America*, 2.

[53]Branch, *Parting the Waters*, 143-200.

[54]Frazier and Lincoln, *The Negro Church in America*, 176.

2. ON THE BATTLEFIELD

[1]Sarah Pruitt, "Broken Treaties With Native American Tribes: Timeline," History.com, November 10, 2020, www.history.com/news/native-american-broken-treaties.

[2]Christopher Watkin, *Biblical Critical Theory: How the Bible's Unfolding Story Makes Sense of Modern Life and Culture* (Grand Rapids, MI: Zondervan Academic, 2022), 183; D. A. Carson, "Where Wrath and Mercy Meet," in *Deep Impact: The Power of the Cross Today*, ed. Hilary Price (Carlisle, Cumbria, UK: OM, 1999), 243.

[3]Watkin, *Biblical Critical Theory*, 183; Carson, "Where Wrath and Mercy Meet," 243.

[4]Earth, Wind & Fire, "Reasons," by Bailey, Philip, Stepney, Charles, Maurice, White, *That's the Way of the World*, Columbia Records, 1974.

[5]Vera Bergengruen, "The United States of Political Violence," *Time*, November 4, 2022, https://time.com/6227754/political-violence-us-states-midterms-2022/.

[6]"Views of American Democracy and Society and Support for Political Violence: First Report from a Nationwide Population-Representative Survey," medRxiv, July 19, 2022, www.medrxiv.org/content/10.1101/2022.07.15.22277693v1.full; Kaleigh Rogers and Zoha Qamar, "What Americans Think About Political Violence," *FiveThirtyEight*, November 4, 2022, https://fivethirtyeight.com/features/what-americans-think-about-political-violence/.

[7]Charles Marsh, *The Beloved Community* (New York: Basic Books, 2008), 4.

[8]Charlie Dates, *Donald Parson and the Understudied Burden of Biblical Black Preaching* (PhD diss., Trinity Evangelical Divinity School, 2017), 96.

[9]Dale Carnegie, *How to Win Friends and Influence People* (New York: Pocket Books, 1936), 8.

[10]Christopher Spata, "No Jail for 'Frothing' Capitol Rioter Who Faced Mental Health Struggle," *Tampa Bay Times*, December 12, 2022, www.tampabay.com/news/crime/2022/12/12/doom-guy-matthew-council-january-6-capitol-riot-sentence-football-cte/.

[11]Genette Cordova, "Destruction Caused by White Rioters Is Being Widely Acknowledged, but Are There Ulterior Motives?" Revolt, June 2, 2020, www.revolt.tv/article/2020-06-02/75737/destruction-caused-by-white-rioters-is-being-widely-acknowledged-but-are-there-ulterior-motives.

[12]Andrew M. Manis, *A Fire You Can't Put Out: The Civil Rights Life of Birmingham's Reverend Fred Shuttlesworth* (Tuscaloosa, AL: University of Alabama Press, 1999), 150-58; Justin E. Giboney, "Rattlesnakes Don't Commit Suicide," *Christianity Today*, June 18, 2024, www.christianitytoday.com/2024/06/rattlesnakes-juneteenth-fred-shuttlesworth-civil-rights/.

[13]Manis, *A Fire You Can't Put Out*, 150-58.

[14]Manis, *A Fire You Can't Put Out*, 150-58.

[15]Patrick Joseph Buchanan, "Culture War Speech: Address to the Republican National Convention," August 17, 1992, https://voicesofdemocracy.umd.edu/buchanan-culture-war-speech-speech-text/.

[16]Mario Cuomo, 1992 Democratic Convention Nomination Speech," C-SPAN, July 15, 1992, www.c-span.org/program/public-affairs-event/democratic-convention-nomination-speech/155486.

[17]James D. Hunter, *Culture Wars: The Struggle to Define America* (New York: Basic Books, 1991), 42.

[18]Hunter, *Culture Wars*, 50.

[19]Hunter, *Culture Wars*, 52.

[20]Hunter, *Culture Wars*, 70.

[21]Encyclopedia.com, s.v. "anti-Catholicism," accessed March 10, 2025, www.encyclopedia.com/history/encyclopedias-almanacs-transcripts-and-maps/anti-catholicism.

[22]Jonathan D. Sarna, "Anti-Semitism and American History," *Commentary* 71, no. 3 (March 1981), 43.

[23]Hunter, *Culture Wars*, 70.

[24]Hunter, *Culture Wars*, 71, 76-78.

[25]Brand Blanshard, "Rationalism," *Britannica*, November 22, 2024, www.britannica.com/topic/rationalism.

[26]Jean-Jacques Rousseau, *The Social Contract* (New York: Penguin Books, 2004), i.

[27]Friedrich Nietzsche, *Beyond Good and Evil* (Garden City, NY: Dover Publications, 1998).

[28]Sigmund Freud, "Three Essays on the Theory of Sexuality," in *The Standard Edition of the Complete Psychological Works of Sigmund Freud*, ed. J. Strachey, vol. 7 (London: Hogarth Press, 1905), 125-245.

[29]Hunter, *Culture Wars*, 79.

[30]John G. Machen, *Christianity and Liberalism* (Warrendale, PA: Ichthus Publications, 1923), 184.

[31]Machen, *Christianity and Liberalism*, 7.

[32]"John Gresham Machen," *Encyclopedia Britannica*, accessed December 16, 2024, www.britannica.com/biography/John-Gresham-Machen.

[33]Hunter, *Culture Wars*, 100.

[34]Eric Schaefer, *Sex Scene: Media and the Sexual Revolution* (Durham, NC: Duke Press, 2004), 3.

[35]"The Pill and the Sexual Revolution," PBS: American Experience, accessed December 17, 2024, www.pbs.org/wgbh/americanexperience/features/pill-and-sexual-revolution/.

[36]Audiey Kao, "History of Oral Contraception," *AMA Journal of Ethics*, June 2000, https://journalofethics.ama-assn.org/article/history-oral-contraception/2000-06.

[37]Kao, "History of Oral Contraception."

[38]Schaefer, *Sex Scene*, 3.

[39]Schaefer, *Sex Scene*, 6.

[40]Schaefer, *Sex Scene*, 5.

[41]Encyclopedia.com, s. v. "sexual revolution," accessed March 10, 2025, www.encyclopedia.com/media/encyclopedias-almanacs-transcripts-and-maps/sexual-revolution.

[42]Schaefer, *Sex Scene*, 7.

[43]Johannah Cornblatt, "A Brief History of Sex Ed in America," *Newsweek*, October 27, 2009, www.newsweek.com/brief-history-sex-ed-america-81001.

[44]Jonathan Merritt, "The Religious Right Turns 33: What Have We Learned?," *The Atlantic*, June 8, 2012, www.theatlantic.com/politics/archive/2012/06/the-religious-right-turns-33-what-have-we-learned/258204/; *Encyclopedia Britannica*, s. v. "moral majority," by Amy Tikkanen, accessed on December 16, 2024, www.britannica.com/topic/Moral-Majority.

[45]Andy Hoglund, "Flashback: Hustler Magazine Scores First Amendment Victory Against Jerry Falwell," *Rolling Stone*, February 10, 2021, www.rollingstone.com/culture/culture-news/flashback-hustler-magazine-scores-first-amendment-victory-against-jerry-falwell-128956/.

[46]Merritt, "The Religious Right Turns 33."

[47]Tikkanen, "moral majority."

[48]James H. Davis, "How America's Culture Wars Have Evolved into a Class War," *The Washington Post*, September 12, 2017, www.washingtonpost.com/news/posteverything/wp/2017/09/12/how-americas-culture-wars-have-evolved-into-a-class-war/; Zack Stanton, "How the Culture War Could Break Democracy," *Politico*, May 20, 2021, www.politico.com/news/magazine/2021/05/20/culture-war-politics-2021-democracy-analysis-489900.

[49]"The Hidden Tribes of America," Hidden Tribes, accessed March 10, 2025, https://hiddentribes.us/.

[50]"The Hidden Tribes of America."

[51]Andrew Martin, *Grimke: On the Christian Life* (Wheaton, IL: Crossway, 2025), 195.

[52]*The Words of Gardner Taylor*, compiled by Edward L. Taylor, vol. 2, *Sermons from the Middle Years, 1970–1980* (Valley Forge, PA: Judson Press, 2000), 118-19.

[53]May Beth Swetnam Mathews, *Doctrine and Race: African American Evangelicals and Fundamentalism Between the Wars* (Tuscaloosa, AL: University of Alabama Press, 2017), 2.

[54]Mary R. Sawyer, "Black Protestantism as Expressed in Ecumenical Activity," in *Re-forming the Center: American Protestantism, 1900 to the Present*, ed. Douglas Jacobsen and Williams Vance Trollinger (Grand Rapids, MI: Eerdsman, 1998), 284-85.

[55]Mathews, *Doctrine and Race*, 7.

[56]Mathews, *Doctrine and Race*, 5.

[57]Andrew Hartman, *A History of the Culture Wars—A War for the Soul of America* (Chicago: University of Chicago Press, 2015).

[58]Seymour M. Lipset, "The Activists: A Profile," *National Affairs*, The Public Interest Fall 1968, 47; Yuval Levin, *A Time To Build* (New York: Basic Books, 2020), 113.

[59]Devon V. Maldonado, "Did the Hippies Have Nothing to Say?," *BBC*, May 29, 2018, www.bbc.com/culture/article/20180529-did-the-hippies-have-nothing-to-say.

[60]Eldridge Cleaver, *Soul on Ice* (New York: Dell Publishing, 1968), 103.

[61]Mathews, *Doctrine and Race*, 1.

[62]Karl Vick and Ashley Surdin, "Most Calif. Blacks Backed Proposition 8," *NBC News*, November 7, 2008, www.nbcnews.com/id/wbna27584685.

[63]Richard H. Cain, "All We Ask Is Equal Laws, Equal Legislation and Equal Rights (US House of Representatives, January 10, 1874)," Black Past, January 28, 2007, www.blackpast.org/african-american-history/1874-richard-harvey-cain-all-we-ask-equal-laws-equal-legislation-and-equal-rights/.

3. A WRETCH LIKE ME

[1]Alice Walser, "Can't Hate Anybody and See God's Face," *New York Times*, April 29, 1973, www.nytimes.com/1973/04/29/archives/fannie-lou-hamer-cant-hate-anybody-and-see-gods-face.html.

[2]Meg Kinnard and Denise Lavoie, "Court Upholds Death Sentence for Church Shooter Dylann Roof," *Associated Press*, August 25, 2021, https://apnews.com/article/religion-389bcc56019f268cb1056e37a517bd6c; www.history.com/this-day-in-history/charleston-ame-church-shooting.

[3]Kinnard and Lavoie, "Court Upholds Death Sentence."

[4]Mark Berman, "I Forgive You. Relatives of Charleston Church Shooting Victims Address Dylann Roof," *Washington Post*, June 19, 2015, www.washingtonpost.com/news/post-nation/wp/2015/06/19/i-forgive-you-relatives-of-charleston-church-victims-address-dylann-roof/.

[5]German Lopez, "The Reagan Administration's Unbelievable Response to the HIV/AIDS Epidemic," Vox, December 1, 2016, www.vox.com/2015/12/1/9828348/ronald-reagan-hiv-aids.

[6]"The HIV/AIDS Epidemic in the United States: The Basics," KFF, August, 16, 2024, www.kff.org/hivaids/fact-sheet/the-hivaids-epidemic-in-the-united-states-the-basics/#footnote-525108-3.

[7]Roxanne Roberts, “Hillary Clinton’s ‘Deplorables’ Speech Shocked Voters Five Years Ago—But Some Feel It Was Prescient,” *Washington Post*, August 31, 2021, www.washingtonpost.com/lifestyle/2021/08/31/deplorables-basket-hillary-clinton/.

[8]Jeffrey E. Miller, “Tax Collector,” in *The Lexham Bible Dictionary*, ed. John D. Barry et al. (Bellingham, WA: Lexham Press, 2016).

[9]Douglas Stuart, “Jonah,” in *New Bible Commentary: 21st Century Edition*, ed. D. A. Carson et al., 4th ed. (Downers Grove, IL: InterVarsity Press, 1994), 814.

[10]Brian Duignan, “Manichaeism,” *Encyclopedia Britannica*, accessed December 16, 2024, www.britannica.com/topic/Manichaeism.

[11]Arthur C. Brooks, *Love Your Enemies: How Decent People Can Save America from the Culture of Contempt* (New York: Broadside Books, 2019), 21.

[12]Charles Taylor, *A Secular Age* (Belknap Press, 2018), 698.

[13]Martin Luther King Jr., “Facing the Challenge of a New Age,” in *A Testament of Hope: The Essential Writings and Speeches of Martin Luther King Jr.*, ed. James M. Washington (New York: Harper San Francisco, 1991), 140.

[14]Taylor Branch, *Parting the Waters: America in the King Years, 1954–1963* (New York: Simon & Schuster, 1988), 22-23.

[15]Aleksandr Solzhenitsyn, *The Gulag Archipelago* (London: Vintage Classics, 2018), part 4, chap. 1, “The Ascent.”

[16]Kay Mills, *This Little Light of Mine* (Lexington: University Press of Kentucky, 2007), 60.

[17]Bernard Lafayette Jr., “Nonviolence and the Chicago Freedom Movement,” in *The Chicago Freedom Movement: Martin Luther King, Jr. and Civil Rights Activism in the North*, ed. Mary Lou Finley et al. (Lexington: University Press of Kentucky, 2016), 538.

[18]Nannie H. Burroughs, *H. Nannie Helen Burroughs: A Documentary Portrait of an Early Civil Rights Pioneer 1900–1959*, ed. and annotated by Kelisha B. Graves (Notre Dame, IN: University of Notre Dame Press, 2019), xxxi.

[19]Jerry A. Johnson, “Image of God,” ed. Chad Brand et al., *Holman Illustrated Bible Dictionary* (Nashville, TN: Holman Bible Publishers, 2003), 806.

[20]Stanley J. Grenz and Jay T. Smith, *Pocket Dictionary of Ethics* (Downers Grove, IL: InterVarsity Press, 2003), 58.

[21]Michael S. Heiser, “Image of God,” in *The Lexham Bible Dictionary*, ed. John D. Barry et al. (Bellingham, WA: Lexham Press, 2016).

[22]Zack Stanton, “How the Culture War Could Break Democracy,” *Politico*, May 20, 2021, www.politico.com/news/magazine/2021/05/20/culture-war-politics-2021-democracy-analysis-489900.

[23]Martin Luther King Jr., "Letter from a Birmingham Jail [King, Jr.]," African Studies Center, University of Pennsylvania, accessed Dec. 16, 2024, www.africa.upenn.edu/Articles_Gen/Letter_Birmingham.html.

[24]Leon Morris, *Luke: An Introduction and Commentary*, vol. 3, *Tyndale New Testament Commentaries* (Downers Grove, IL: InterVarsity Press, 1988), 206.

4. GETTING THE SPIRIT

[1]Martin Luther King Jr., "Letter from a Birmingham Jail [King, Jr.]," African Studies Center, University of Pennsylvania, accessed Dec. 16, 2024, www.africa.upenn.edu/Articles_Gen/Letter_Birmingham.html.

[2]William A. Jones, "Where the Trumpet Is Expected, the Flute Will Not Suffice," Bethany Baptist Church, Brooklyn, NY, February 4, 2015, video, 8:53, www.youtube.com/watch?v=df5fSAf_LIo.

[3]"Watts Riots," Civil Rights Digital Library, accessed December 16, 2024, https://crdl.usg.edu/events/watts_riots; "Watts Rebellion," History.com, June 24, 2020, www.history.com/topics/1960s/watts-riots.

[4]"Watts Riots"; "Watts Rebellion."

[5]Martin Luther King Jr., "Watts Rebellion (Los Angeles)," Address at the Chicago Freedom Festival, March 12, 1966, CULC-ICIU, The Martin Luther King, Jr. Research and Education Institute, accessed December 16, 2024, https://kinginstitute.stanford.edu/watts-rebellion-los-angeles.

[6]Samuel D. Proctor and William D. Watley, *Sermons from the Black Pulpit* (Valley Forge, PA: Judson Press, 2014), 59.

[7]Proctor and Watley, *Sermons from the Black Pulpit*, 62.

[8]Robert A. Caro, *The Power Broker: Robert Moses and the Fall of New York* (New York: Knopf, 1974).

[9]Joseph Carroll, "Family Values Important to Presidential Vote," Gallup, December 26, 2007, https://news.gallup.com/poll/103375/public-family-values-important-presidential-vote.aspx.

[10]Mark Morford, "The Sad, Quotable Jerry Falwell / It's Bad Form to Speak Ill of the Dead. Good Thing This Man's Own Vile Words Speak for Themselves," SFGate, May 18, 2007, www.sfgate.com/entertainment/morford/article/The-Sad-Quotable-Jerry-Falwell-It-s-bad-form-3302297.php.

[11]C. A. W. Clark, "Spiritual Bankruptcy," sermon, Good Street Baptist Church, Dallas, TX, June 1, 2023, video, 28:57, https://youtu.be/JPOVyw799v8?si=_A_Xp_vLooiuXCSO.

[12]Jim Jones, "Jim Jones preaching at a Peoples Temple Meeting in 1971," April 14, 2019, video, 29:34, www.youtube.com/watch?v=bKwcFlM6kiU.

[13]"Jonestown: The Life and Death of Peoples Temple," PBS—American Experience, accessed December 16, 2024, www.pbs.org/wgbh/americanexperience/features/jonestown-bio-jones/.

[14]Alison Eldridge, "Jonestown," *Encyclopedia Britannica*, accessed December 15, 2024, www.britannica.com/event/Jonestown.

[15]Proctor and Watley, *Sermons from the Black Pulpit*, 59.

[16]Christine Zhu, "Jasmine Crockett Backs Claim Calling Marjorie Taylor Greene Racist," *Politico*, May 19, 2024, www.politico.com/news/2024/05/19/jasmine-crockett-backs-claim-calling-mtg-racist-00158792.

[17]Nannie H. Burroughs, *Nannie Helen Burroughs: A Documentary Portrait of an Early Civil Rights Pioneer 1900–1959*, ed. and annotated by Kelisha B. Graves (Notre Dame, IN: University of Notre Dame Press. 2019), xxi-xxvii, 53-63.

[18]Burroughs, *Nannie Helen Burroughs*, xxvii.

[19]Burroughs, *Nannie Helen Burroughs*, 169.

[20]Burroughs, *Nannie Helen Burroughs*, 88.

[21]Jasmine L. Holmes, *Carved in Ebony: Lessons from the Black Women Who Shape Us* (Minneapolis: Bethany House Publishers, 2021), 56.

[22]"Reconstruction in America: Racial Violence after the Civil War, 1865–1876," Equal Justice Initiative, accessed December 17, 2024, https://eji.org/report/reconstruction-in-america/documenting-reconstruction-violence/#34-documented-mass-lynchings-during-the-reconstruction-era.

[23]"Tulsa Race Riot of 1921," Tulsa City-County Library, accessed December 17, 2024, www.tulsalibrary.org/tulsa-race-riot-1921.

[24]German Lopez, "The Long History of Attacks Against Civil Rights Organizations," Vox, January 9, 2015, www.vox.com/2015/1/9/7520529/history-colorado-bombing.

[25]"Black Church Burnings," PBS—This Far by Faith, accessed December 17, 2024, www.pbs.org/thisfarbyfaith/journey_5/p_4.html.

[26]*Mahalia Jackson: The Glory & the Power*, directed by Jeff Scheftel, narrated by Paul Winfield (Xenon, 1997), DVD.

[27]Pamela Garfield-Jaeger, "From De-stigmatizing to Normalizing Mental Illness," Pamela's Newletter, January 7, 2023, https://pamthetruthfultherapist.substack.com/p/from-de-stigmatizing-to-normalizing.

[28]Jen Doll, "Trigger Warnings on Classic Literature Are One Small Step from Book Banning," *The Guardian*, May 20, 2014, www.theguardian.com/commentisfree/2014/may/20/trigger-warnings-college-campus-books.

[29]Jonathan Haidt and Greg Lukianoff, *The Coddling of the American Mind* (New York: Penguin Press, 2018), 20-25; Jonathan Haidt and Greg Lukianoff, "The

Coddling of the American Mind," *The Atlantic*, September 2015, www.theatlantic.com/magazine/archive/2015/09/the-coddling-of-the-american-mind/399356/.

[30]Taylor Branch, *Parting the Waters: America in the King Years 1954–65* (New York: Simon & Schuster Paperbacks, 1988), 532.

[31]Zach Mills, *The Last Blues Preacher* (Minneapolis: Fortress Press, 2018), 206-7.

[32]Mills, *Last Blues Preacher*, 210.

[33]Kate Julian, "What Happened to American Childhood?," *The Atlantic*, May 2020, www.theatlantic.com/magazine/archive/2020/05/childhood-in-an-anxious-age/609079/.

[34]Haidt and Lukianoff, *The Coddling of the American Mind*, 24-26. Jonathan Haidt and Greg Lukianoff, "The Safety Police: Is Free Speech Being Stifled on College Campus," NYU|Stern, August 15, 2019, www.stern.nyu.edu/experience-stern/faculty-research/safety-police-free-speech-being-stifled-college-campuses.

[35]Haidt and Lukianoff, *The Coddling of the American Mind*, 24-26.

[36]Marvin Winans, "I Feel Like Going On," track 4 on *The Gospel Music Celebration Pt. 1: Tribute to Bishop G.E. Patterson*, INgrooves (on behalf of World Class Gospel), 2010, compact disk.

5. JESUS, YOU'RE THE CENTER

[1]Mary R. Sawyer, *Black Ecumenism: Implementing the Demands of Justice* (Valley Forge, PA: Trinity Press International, 1994), 16-19.

[2]Sawyer, *Black Ecumenism*, 21.

[3]Sawyer, *Black Ecumenism*, 21.

[4]Sawyer, *Black Ecumenism*, 29.

[5]Sawyer, *Black Ecumenism*, xiii.

[6]Sawyer, *Black Ecumenism*, 10.

[7]"Nixon's Record on Civil Rights," Richard Nixon Foundation, August 4, 2017, www.nixonfoundation.org/2017/08/nixons-record-civil-rights-2/.

[8]"J. C. Watts, Only Black Republic in Congress, Calls It Quits," OU Daily, July 2, 2002, www.oudaily.com/j-c-watts-only-black-republican-in-congress-calls-its-quits/article_42ca0468-f5a3-5b33-b10d-63449e862f81.html.

[9]Charlie Dates, *Donald Parson and the Understudied Burden of Biblical Black Preaching* (PhD diss., Trinity Evangelical Divinity School, 2017), 148.

[10]Dates, *Donald Parson*, 113; Rene C. Padilla, *What Is Integral Mission?* (Minneapolis: Fortress Press. 2021), 1-25.

[11]Dates, *Donald Parson*, 115.

[12]Martin Luther King Jr., "Letter from a Birmingham Jail [King, Jr.]," African Studies Center, University of Pennsylvania, accessed Dec. 16, 2024, www.africa.upenn.edu/Articles_Gen/Letter_Birmingham.html

[13]King Jr., "Letter from a Birmingham Jail."

[14]Jeanne Theoharis, "Martin Luther King and the Polite Racism of White Liberals," *Washington Post*, January 17, 2020, www.washingtonpost.com/nation/2020/01/17/martin-luther-king-polite-racism-white-liberals/.

[15]Gilbert E. Patterson, "Sermon at Temple of Deliverance Church of God in Christ," November 27, 2023, video, 0:56, www.youtube.com/watch?v=PfLFww2R5Pc.

[16]Justin E. Giboney, "The Selfish Ambition of the Immigration Debate," *Christianity Today*, February 8, 2024, www.christianitytoday.com/ct/2024/february-web-only/selfish-ambition-of-our-immigration-debate.html.

[17]*The Britannica Dictionary*, s. v. "Tribalism," accessed December 17, 2024, www.britannica.com/dictionary/tribalism.

[18]Thomas L. Friedman, "Have We Reshaped Middle East Politics or Started to Mimic It?," *New York Times*, September 14, 2021, www.nytimes.com/2021/09/14/opinion/america-democracy-middle-east-tribalism.html.

[19]Justin E. Giboney, "Transcending the Blame Game," *Liberty Magazine*, March/April 2022, www.libertymagazine.org/article/transcending-the-blame-game.

[20]Alan I. Abramowitz and Steven Webster, "The Only Thing We Have to Fear Is the Other Party," The Center for Politics, June 4, 2015, https://centerforpolitics.org/crystalball/articles/the-only-thing-we-have-to-fear-is-the-other-party/.

[21]Abramowitz and Webster, "The Only Thing We Have to Fear."

[22]Abramowitz and Webster, "The Only Thing We Have to Fear."

[23]Jessica Taylor, "Mitt Romney Finally Takes Credit for Obamacare," NPR, October 23, 2015, www.npr.org/sections/itsallpolitics/2015/10/23/451200436/mitt-romney-finally-takes-credit-for-obamacare.

[24]Taylor, "Mitt Romney Finally Takes Credit for Obamacare."

[25]Jonathan Haidt, "Why the Past 10 Years of American Life Have Been Uniquely Stupid," *The Atlantic*, April 11, 2022, www.theatlantic.com/magazine/archive/2022/05/social-media-democracy-trust-babel/629369/.

[26]*Encyclopedia Britannica Online*, s. v. "The North Star," by Melissa Petruzzello, accessed December 17, 2024, www.britannica.com/topic/The-North-Star-American-newspaper.

[27]Giboney, "Transcending the Blame Game."

[28]Walter Hooper, *The Collected Letters of C.S. Lewis, Volume 2 (Letter to Arthur Greeves on 12/29/1935)* (New York: HarperCollins, 2004), 170.

[29]Bonnie Kristian, *Untrustworthy: The Knowledge Crisis Breaking Our Brains, Polluting Our Politics, and Corrupting Christian Community* (Grand Rapids, MI: Brazos Press, 2022), 15.

[30]Hannah Arendt, *The Origins of Totalitarianism* (1951; repr. New York: Harcourt Brace Jovanovich, 1973), 382; Kristian, *Untrustworthy*, 17.

[31]Brian Resnick, "There May Be an Antidote to Politically Motivated Reasoning. And It's Wonderfully Simple," Vox, February 7, 2017, www.vox.com/science-and-health/2017/2/1/14392290/partisan-bias-dan-kahan-curiosity.

[32]Haidt, "Why the Past 10 Years of American Life Have Been Uniquely Stupid."

[33]Justin E. Giboney, "Today's Mob Mentality Politics: Just Deny It, and Keep Moving," *The Hill*, September 6, 2020, https://thehill.com/opinion/campaign/515156-todays-mob-mentality-politics-just-deny-it-and-keep-moving/.

[34]Sawyer, *Black Ecumenism*, 37.

[35]"Montgomery Improvement Association Press Release, Bus Protesters Call Southern Negro Leaders Conference on Transportation and Nonviolent Integration," The Martin Luther King, Jr. Research and Education Institute, January 7, 1957 https://kinginstitute.stanford.edu/king-papers/documents/montgomery-improvement-association-press-release-bus-protesters-call-southern.

[36]"Southern Christian Leadership Conference," The Martin Luther King, Jr. Research and Education Institute, January 10, 1957, https://kinginstitute.stanford.edu/encyclopedia/southern-christian-leadership-conference-sclc.

[37]"A Statement to the South and Nation," issued by the Southern Negro Leaders Conference on Transportation and Nonviolent Integration, January 10, 1957, https://kinginstitute.stanford.edu/king-papers/documents/statement-south-and-nation-issued-southern-negro-leaders-conference.

[38]"A Statement to the South and Nation."

6. WE ARE SHARING

[1]Frederick Douglass, "What to the Slave Is the Fourth of July?," Constitution Center, accessed December 17, 2024, https://constitutioncenter.org/the-constitution/historic-document-library/detail/frederick-douglass-what-to-the-slave-is-the-fourth-of-july-1852.

[2]Douglass, "What to the Slave Is the Fourth of July?"

[3]"AND Campaign 2023 Statement," AND Campaign, April 5, 2023, https://andcampaign.org/press/and-campaign-2023-statement/.

[4]Stephen E. Ambrose, "Founding Fathers and Slaveholders," *Smithsonian Magazine*, November 2002, www.smithsonianmag.com/history/founding-fathers-and-slaveholders-72262393/.

[5]Hiram R. Revels, "(1871) Revels Urges Desegregation of District of Columbia School," senatorial address in the United States Senate, January 28, 2007, www.blackpast.org/african-american-history/1871-senator-hiram-revels-calls-end-segregated-schools.

[6]Kevin Eckstrom, "Blacks Say Atheists Were Unseen Civil Rights Heroes," Religion News, February 22, 2012, https://religionnews.com/2012/02/22/blacks-say-atheists-were-unseen-civil-rights-heroes/.

[7]Joshua Eaton and Lexi McMenemin, "How Bayard Rustin's Quaker, AME Faith Shaped the Civil Rights Era." *Sojourners*, July 26, 2021, https://sojo.net/articles/how-bayard-rustin-s-quaker-ame-faith-shaped-civil-rights-era; Jim Axelrod, "A Rabbi's Moment at the March on Washington," *CBS News*, August 31, 2013, www.cbsnews.com/news/a-rabbis-moment-at-the-march-on-washington/; "Official Program for the March on Washington," National Archives, accessed December 17, 2024, www.archives.gov/milestone-documents/official-program-for-the-march-on-washington.

[8]MacKenzie Weinger, "Study: Red States More Charitable," *Politico*, August 20, 2012, www.politico.com/story/2012/08/study-red-states-more-charitable-079888; Nicholas Kristof, "Conservatives Are More Giving Than Liberals," *Seattle Times*, December 26, 2008, www.seattletimes.com/opinion/conservatives-are-more-giving-than-liberals/; Mark Clark, "A Response to the Objection That Christian Are Pro-Birth, Not Pro-Life," Reasons to Believe, July 21, 2022, https://reasons.org/explore/blogs/voices/a-response-to-the-objection-that-christians-are-pro-birth-not-pro-life.

[9]"Black Power," The Martin Luther King, Jr. Research and Education Institute, accessed December 17, 2024, https://kinginstitute.stanford.edu/black-power.

[10]Jasmine L. Holmes, *Carved in Ebony: Lessons from the Black Women Who Shape Us* (Minneapolis: Bethany House Publishers, 2021), 56.

[11]Nannie H. Burroughs, *Nannie Helen Burroughs: A Documentary Portrait of an Early Civil Rights Pioneer 1900–1959*, ed. and annotated by Kelisha B. Graves (Notre Dame, IN: University of Notre Dame Press. 2019), xxi.

[12]Burroughs, *Nannie Helen Burroughs*, 169.

[13]Burroughs, *Nannie Helen Burroughs*, 88.

[14]Burroughs, *Nannie Helen Burroughs*, xv-xxix.

7. AIN'T THAT GOOD NEWS

[1]"The Double V Victory," The National WWII Museum, accessed December 17, 2024, www.nationalww2museum.org/war/articles/double-v-victory.

[2]Erin Blakemore, "How the GI Bill's Promise Was Denied to a Million Black WWII Veterans," History.com, June 21 2019, www.history.com/news/gi-bill-black-wwii-veterans-benefits.

[3]Blakemore, "How the GI Bill's Promise Was Denied."

[4]John Wake, "The Shocking Truth 50 Years After the 1968 Fair Housing Act: The Black Homeownership Paradox." *Forbes*, January 7, 2021, www.forbes.com/sites/johnwake/2019/05/16/the-shocking-truth-about-the-u-s-black-homeownership-rate-50-years-after-the-1968-fair-housing-act/.

[5]"Chicago Campaign," The Martin Luther King, Jr. Research and Education Institute, January 7, 1966, https://kinginstitute.stanford.edu/chicago-campaign#:~:text=On%207%20January%201966%2C%20Martin,the%20South%20to%20northern%20cities.

[6]*Mahalia Jackson: The Glory & the Power*, directed by Jeff Scheftel, narrated by Paul Winfield (Xenon, 1997), DVD.

[7]"Public Spectacle Lynchings," Equal Justice Initiative, February 14, 2018, https://eji.org/news/history-racial-injustice-public-spectacle-lynchings/.

[8]"Public Spectacle Lynchings."

[9]Tom Gjelten, "White Supremacist Ideas Have Historical Roots in U.S. Christianity," NPR, July 1, 2020, www.npr.org/2020/07/01/883115867/white-supremacist-ideas-have-historical-roots-in-u-s-christianity.

[10]Gjelten, "White Supremacist Ideas Have Historical Roots."

[11]Gjelten, "White Supremacist Ideas Have Historical Roots"; "Transcript of a Public Meeting Held by the Montgomery County Citizens Council at Garrett Coliseum," Alabama Department of Archives & History, June 8, 1961, https://digital.archives.alabama.gov/digital/collection/voices/id/3215.

[12]David A. Hollinger, "One Drop & One Hate," Daedalus, Winter 2005, www.amacad.org/publication/one-drop-one-hate.

[13]"Working Together to Reduce Black Maternal Mortality," Centers for Disease Control, April 8, 2024, www.cdc.gov/womens-health/features/maternal-mortality.html.

[14]"Working Together to Reduce Black Maternal Mortality."

[15]Ben Lillie, "All Our Survival Is Tied to the Survival of Everyone: Bryan Stevenson at TED2012," TED, March 1, 2012, https://blog.ted.com/all-of-our-survival-is-tied-to-the-survival-of-everyone-bryan-stevenson-at-ted2012/#:~:text=And%20yet%20here%20in%20this,if%20the%20defendant%20is%20black.&text=Our%20whole%20identity%20is%20at%20risk.

[16]"White Christians Have Become Even Less Motivated to Address Racial Injustice," Barna Group, September 15, 2020, www.barna.com/research/american-christians-race-problem/.

[17]"White Christians Have Become Even Less Motivated."

[18]Taylor Branch, *Parting the Waters: America in the King Years 1954–63* (New York: Simon & Schuster Paperbacks, 1988), 339-40.

[19]Russell Moore, "The American Evangelical Church Is in Crisis. There's Only One Way Out," *The Atlantic*, July 25, 2023, www.theatlantic.com/ideas/archive/2023/07/christian-evangelical-church-division-politics/674810/.

[20]Mark Wingfield, "Jeffress Says He's Not a 'Christian Nationalist' but America Was Founded as a 'Christian Nation,'" Baptist News, July 5, 2022, https://baptistnews.com/article/jeffress-says-hes-not-a-christian-nationalist-but-america-was-founded-as-a-christian-nation/.

[21]Rodney Kennedy, "Flynn Tells Preachers, 'Put the Bible Aside and Read the Constitution,'" Baptist News, August 14, 2023, https://baptistnews.com/article/flynn-tells-preachers-put-the-bible-aside-and-read-the-constitution/.

[22]Mary C. Terrell, "What It Means to Be Colored in the Capital of the United States," Iowa State University, Archives of Women's Political Communication, October 10, 1906.

[23]Caroline M. Elkins, *Legacy of Violence: A History of the British Empire* (New York: Alfred A. Knopf, 2022).

[24]Martin Luther King, "The Other America," Beacon Broadside, March 10, 1968, www.beaconbroadside.com/broadside/2018/03/martin-luther-king-jrs-the-other-america-still-radical-50-years-later.html; www.youtube.com/watch?v=dOWDtDUKz-U.

[25]Paul D. Miller, "What is Christian Nationalism?," *Christianity Today*, February 3, 2021, www.christianitytoday.com/ct/2021/february-web-only/what-is-christian-nationalism.html.

[26]Ida B. Wells, "This Awful Slaughter," speech, NAACP 1909, accessed December 17, 2024, www.blackpast.org/african-american-history/1909-ida-b-wells-awful-slaughter/.

[27]Wells, "This Awful Slaughter."

[28]Frederick Douglass, "What to the Slave Is the Fourth of July?," Constitution Center, accessed December 17, 2024, https://constitutioncenter.org/the-constitution/historic-document-library/detail/frederick-douglass-what-to-the-slave-is-the-fourth-of-july-1852.

[29]William Shakespeare, *The Tempest*, Act 2, Scene 1, lines 289-90, 2nd Edition, Folger Shakespeare Library, accessed December 18, 2024, www.folger.edu/explore/shakespeares-works/the-tempest/read/2/1/.

8. YOU WILL SURELY DRIFT AWAY

[1]Emily St. James, "The Sexual Abuse Scandal Rocking the Southern Baptist Convention, Explained," Vox, June 7, 2022, www.vox.com/culture/23131530/southern-baptist-convention-sexual-abuse-scandal-guidepost.

[2]Randall Balmer, "In 'The Exvangelicals,' Sarah McCammon Tells the Tale of Losing Her Religion," *LA Times*, March 20, 2024, www.latimes.com/opinion/story/2024-03-20/white-christian-evangelical-sarah-mccammon-exvangelicals-autobiography.

[3]C. S. Lewis, *Mere Christianity* (New York: HarperCollins, 1972), 186.

[4]May Beth Swetnam Mathews, *Doctrine and Race: African American Evangelicals and Fundamentalism between the Wars* (Tuscaloosa, AL: University of Alabama Press, 2017), 2.

[5]*Mahalia Jackson: The Glory & the Power*, directed by Jeff Scheftel, narrated by Paul Winfield (Xenon, 1997), DVD.

[6]Laurraine Goreau, *Just Mahalia, Baby* (Gretna, LA: Pelican Publishing Company, 1975), 20.

[7]Goreau, *Just Mahalia, Baby*.

[8]*Mahalia Jackson: The Glory & the Power*.

[9]Goreau, *Just Mahalia, Baby*, 23.

[10]Goreau, *Just Mahalia, Baby*, 302.

[11]Goreau, *Just Mahalia, Baby*, 338-39.

[12]Jonathan Haidt, *The Righteous Mind: Why Good People Are Divided by Politics and Religion* (New York: Pantheon Books, 2012), 95-105.; Mark Movsesian, "Weird Values," *First Things* (blog), October 10, 2012, www.firstthings.com/blogs/firstthoughts/2012/10/weird-values.

[13]David Goodhart, "Last Hope for the Left," *Prospect Magazine*, March 19, 2012, www.prospectmagazine.co.uk/culture/50009/last-hope-for-the-left.

[14]"Understanding Sex Work in an Open Society," Open Society Foundation, April 2019, www.opensocietyfoundations.org/explainers/understanding-sex-work-open-society.

[15]Gardner C. Taylor, "It Is Finished," sermon, September 17, 2019, video, 31:07, www.youtube.com/watch?v=cCoZ-Qo3Zpk.

[16]David Brooks, *The Road to Character* (New York: Random House, 2015) 101-2; Justin E. Giboney, "Christian Virtue Strengthens the Social Justice Cause,"

Christianity Today, August 24, 2021, www.christianitytoday.com/ct/2021/august-web-only/racism-social-justice-christian-virtue-strengthens.html.

[17]Brooks, *The Road to Character*, 76-83.

[18]Brooks, *The Road to Character*, 101-3; Giboney, "Christian Virtue Strengthens the Social Justice Cause."

[19]Dan Avery, "Trans Women Retain Athletic Edge After a Year of Hormone Therapy, Study Finds," NBC News, January 5, 2021, www.nbcnews.com/feature/nbc-out/trans-women-retain-athletic-edge-after-year-hormone-therapy-study-n1252764.

[20]Phyllis Garland and Richard Kilberg, "Adam Clayton Powell," Direct Cinema, 1989 (Narrated by Julian Bond).

[21]*Encyclopedia Britannica*, s. v. "Ida B. Wells-Barnett," accessed December 17, 2024, www.britannica.com/biography/Ida-B-Wells-Barnett.

[22]Holly Frey and Tracy V. Wilson, "Ida B. Wells-Barnett," Stuff You Missed in History Class, June 4, 2018, www.iheart.com/podcast/105-stuff-you-missed-in-histor-21124503/episode/ida-b-wells-barnett-29413454/.

[23]Wallace Thurman, *Infants of the Spring* (New York: Dover Publications, 2013), 85.

[24]Matthew Yglesias, "The Great Awokening," Vox, April 1, 2019, www.vox.com/2019/3/22/18259865/great-awokening-white-liberals-race-polling-trump-2020.

[25]Esau McCaulley, *How Far to the Promised Land* (New York: Convergent Books, 2023), 78.

[26]Kiana Cox, "Black Americans' Views on Transgender and Nonbinary Issues," Pew Research, Feb, 16, 2023, www.pewresearch.org/race-ethnicity/2023/02/16/black-americans-views-on-transgender-and-nonbinary-issues/.

[27]Cox, "Black Americans' Views on Transgender and Nonbinary Issues."

[28]Claudia Willen, "All the Celebrities Who Have Signed an Open Letter to Defund Police Budgets," *Business Insider*, June 3, 2020, www.businessinsider.com/celebrities-signed-an-open-letter-to-defund-police-budgets-2020-6.

[29]Lydia Saad, "Black Americans Want Police to Retain Local Presence," Gallup, August 5, 2020, https://news.gallup.com/poll/316571/black-americans-police-retain-local-presence.aspx.

[30]Saad, "Black Americans Want Police to Retain Local Presence."

[31]"Protecting Pride: Defending the Civil Rights of LGBTQ+ Americans," Human Rights Campaign President Kelley Robinson's congressional testimony, U.S. Senate Committee on the Judiciary, June 21, 2023, www.judiciary.senate.gov/protecting-pride-defending-the-civil-rights-of-lgbtq-americans.

[32]Samuel Smith, "Latinos Are Becoming More Secularized the Longer They Live in US, Hispanic Evangelical Leader Warns," Christian Post, February 2, 2018, www.christianpost.com/news/latinos-are-becoming-more-secularized-the-longer-they-live-in-us-hispanic-evangelical-leader-warns.html.

[33]Nathaniel Givens and Terryl Givens, "Secularism as Scapegoat," Deseret News, October 19, 2022, www.deseret.com/magazine/2022/10/19/23361488/secularism-faith-christianity-belief-religious-decline; Charles Taylor, *A Secular Age* (London: Belknap Press, 2007), 25-27.

[34]Larry Charles, *Religulous*, Lionsgate, 2008; "Film: In 'Religulous' Bill Maher Is More Politically Incorrect Than Ever," The Harvard Law Record, October 16, 2008, https://hlrecord.org/film-in-religulous-bill-maher-is-more-politically-incorrect-than-ever/.

[35]Sam Abrams and Amna Khalid, "Are Colleges and Universities Too Liberal? What the Research Says About the Political Composition of Campuses and Campus Climate," Heterodox Academy, October 21, 2020, https://heterodoxacademy.org/blog/are-colleges-and-universities-too-liberal-what-the-research-says-about-the-political-composition-of-campuses-and-campus-climate/.

[36]Kyle Smith, "Bill Maher Blasts Young Progressives: 'The Problem Is That Your Ideas Are Stupid,'" *National Review*, April 26, 2021, www.nationalreview.com/corner/bill-maher-blasts-young-progressives-the-problem-is-that-your-ideas-are-stupid/.

[37]Ashley Carnahan, "Bill Maher's Attack on Woke School 'Indoctrination' Shows How Much Control Dems Have Over Culture: Critics," January 24, 2023, www.foxnews.com/media/bill-mahers-attack-woke-school-indoctrination-how-much-control-democrats-culture-critics.

[38]Big Rube (OutKast) "Liberation," Aquemini, Arista Records, LLC, 1998.

[39]Justin E. Giboney, "Backbone, Mouthpiece, and Good News," *Comment*, December 7, 2023, https://comment.org/backbone-mouthpiece-and-good-news/.

[40]Aja Romano, "The Second Wave of 'Cancel Culture,'" Vox, May 5, 2021, www.vox.com/22384308/cancel-culture-free-speech-accountability-debate.

[41]David Halberstam, "The White Citizens Council: Respectable Means for Unrespectable Ends," *Commentary Magazine*, October 1956, www.commentary.org/articles/david-halberstam/the-white-citizens-councilsrespectable-means-for-unrespectable-ends/.

[42]Saul D. Alinsky, *Rules for Radicals: A Practical Primer for Realistic Radicals* (New York: Vintage Books, 1989) 128.

9. I KNOW THE LORD WILL MAKE A WAY

[1]Cheyenne Flint, "The Reverend's Roots: Rev. Charles Albert Tindley," Edward H. Nabb Research Center for Delmarva History & Culture—Enduring Connections: Exploring Delmarva's Black History, May 25, 2023, https://enduringconnections.salisbury.edu/story/the-reverends-roots-tindley; Dana Kester-McCabe, "Rev. Charles A. Tindley," Delmarva Almanac, February 27, 2016, https://delmarva-almanac.com/heritage/; "Charles Albert Tindley (1851–1933) Grandfather of Gospel Music," Discipleship Ministries—The United Methodist Church, February 2005, www.umcdiscipleship.org/resources/charles-albert-tindley-1851-1933-grandfather-of-gospel-music.

[2]Charles Tindley, "I'll Overcome Some Day," Hymnary.org, accessed December 18, 2024, https://hymnary.org/text/this_world_is_one_great_battlefield.

[3]"We Shall Overcome: The Story Behind the Song," The Kennedy Center, accessed December 18, 2024, www.kennedy-center.org/education/resources-for-educators/classroom-resources/media-and-interactives/media/music/story-behind-the-song/the-story-behind-the-song/we-shall-overcome/.

[4]"We Shall Overcome."

[5]Andrew Manis, *A Fire You Can't Put Out: The Civil Rights Life of Birminghams's Reverend Fred Shuttlesworth* (Tuscaloosa, AL: University of Alabama Press, 1999), 8.

[6]Kester-McCabe, "Rev. Charles A. Tindley."

[7]Flint, "The Reverend's Roots"; Kester-McCabe, "Rev. Charles A. Tindley"; "Charles Albert Tindley (1851–1933) Grandfather of Gospel Music."

[8]Jonathan Eig, *King: A Life* (New York: Farrar, Straus and Giroux, 2023) 259-67.

[9]David Miller, "A Loss for Dr. King—New Negro Roundup: They Yield," *New York Herald Tribune*, December 19, 1961, https://kinginstitute.stanford.edu/albany-movement.

[10]Michael Jackson, "You Can't Win, You Can't Break Even," Charles Smalls, *The Wiz (Original Soundtrack)*, MCA, 1978.

[11]Derrick Bell, "Racial Realism," *Connecticut Law Review* 24, no. 2 (Winter 1992): 363.

[12]Derrick Bell, *Faces at the Bottom of the Well* (New York: Basic Books, 2018) 1-15.

[13]Ta-Nehisi Coates, *Between the World and Me* (New York: Spiegel & Grau, 2015) 70-71; Melvin L. Rogers, Dissent Magazine, July 21, 2015, www.dissentmagazine.org/online_articles/between-world-me-ta-nehisi-coates-review-despair-hope/.

[14]Gardner C. Taylor, "The Preacher's Dialogue," Preaching Today, accessed December 18, 2024, www.preachingtoday.com/your-soul/calling-to-preach/preachers-dialogue.html.

[15]Melvin L. Rogers, "Between Pain and Despair: What Ta-Nehisi Coates Is Missing," Dissent Magazine, July 21, 2015, www.dissentmagazine.org/online_articles/between-world-me-ta-nehisi-coates-review-despair-hope/.

[16]Rogers, "Between Pain and Despair."

[17]Dartunorro Clark and Janell Ross, "The First Step Act Promised Widespread Reform. What Has the Criminal Justice Overhaul Achieved So Far?," NBC News, November 24, 2019, www.nbcnews.com/politics/politics-news/first-step-act-promised-widespread-reform-what-has-criminal-justice-n1079771.

[18]"Black Impact: Consumer Categories Where African Americans Move Markets," Neilson, February 2018, www.nielsen.com/insights/2018/black-impact-consumer-categories-where-african-americans-move-markets/.

[19]Kevin Allen, "Civil Right Pioneer Says Love Fueled the Movement," University of Notre Dame Law School, March 9, 2017, https://law.nd.edu/news-events/news/civil-rights-pioneer-says-love-fueled-the-movement/; www.dictionary.com/e/greek-words-for-love/.

[20]Kirk Carapezza, "More Black Students Are Headed to Medical School, But Finances Are Still a Major Issue," NPR, January 15, 2022, www.npr.org/2022/01/15/1073331377/more-black-students-are-headed-to-medical-school-but-finances-are-still-a-major-.

[21]Clifton H. Johnson, *God Struck Me Dead* (1969; repr., Eugene, OR: Wipf and Stock Publishers, 2010), xxv.

[22]Fred Shuttlesworth, "Oral History Interview with Fred Shuttlesworth," Birmingham Civil Rights Institute, December 19, 2003, video, posted July 21, 2020, 38:54, www.youtube.com/watch?v=gxPurOe1C8E&t=1111s.

[23]Shuttlesworth, "Oral History Interview with Fred Shuttlesworth."

[24]Andrew Martin, *Grimke: On the Christian Life* (Wheaton, IL: Crossway, 2025), 217-18.

[25]Frederick Douglass, *Narrative of the Life of Frederick Douglass, an American Slave* (New York: Signet Books, 1968), 48-51.

[26]Nannie H. Burroughs, *Nannie Helen Burroughs: A Documentary Portrait of an Early Civil Rights Pioneer 1900–1959*, ed. and annotated by Kelisha B. Graves (Notre Dame, IN: University of Notre Dame Press. 2019), 21-22

[27]Burroughs, *Nannie Helen Burroughs*, 21-22.

[28]Francis E. W. Harper, *The Complete Frances Harper* (Berkeley, CA: Mint Editions, 2021), 201-6.

[29]Raphael. G. Warnock, *The Divided Mind of the Black Church* (New York: NYU Press, 2014), 1-13.

[30]Johnson, *God Struck Me Dead*, xxv.

[31]M. J. Lee and Kevin Liptak, "Biden's Political and Personal Evolution on Abortion on Display After Publication of Draft Supreme Court Opinion," CNN, May 3, 2022, www.cnn.com/2022/05/03/politics/joe-biden-abortion-draft-opinion/index.html.

10. GOD DON'T WANT NO COWARD SOLDIER

[1]William A. Jones, "Clergy in Conflict," sermon at Bethany Baptist Church, Brooklyn, NY—The Bethany Hour, accessed December 18, 2024, https://brooklyn.illumira.net/show.php?pid=njcore:180570.

[2]G. K. Chesterton, *Orthodoxy* (Chicago: Moody Publishers, 2009) 140-41.

[3]"International Civil Rights Walk of Fame—Rev. Fred Shuttlesworth," National Park Service—U.S. Department of the Interior, accessed December 18, 2024, www.nps.gov/features/malu/feat0002/wof/fred_shuttlesworth.htm.

[4]Andrew Manis, *A Fire You Can't Put Out: The Civil Rights Life of Birmingham's Reverend Fred Shuttlesworth* (Tuscaloosa, AL: University of Alabama Press, 1999), 42-44.

[5]Alden Whitman, "Mahalia Jackson, Gospel Singer, and a Civil Rights Symbol, Dies," *New York Times*, January 28, 1972, https://archive.nytimes.com/www.nytimes.com/learning/general/onthisday/bday/1026.html.

[6]Frances E. W. Harper, *The Complete Frances Harper* (Berkeley: Mint Edition, 2021), 73, 191.

[7]Harper, *The Complete Frances Harper*, 36.

[8]Harper, *The Complete Frances Harper*, 194.

[9]"Frances Ellen Watkins Harper," Maryland Commission for Women, accessed December 18, 2024, https://msa.maryland.gov/msa/educ/exhibits/womenshallfame/html/harper.html; Harper, *The Complete Frances Harper*, 165.

[10]"Mildred Jefferson," Schlesinger Library/Collections—Harvard Radcliffe Institute, accessed December 29, 2024, www.radcliffe.harvard.edu/schlesinger-library/collections/mildred-jefferson.

[11]Joshua Prager, "Opinion: The Groundbreaking and Complicated Life of Mildred Fay Jefferson," *The Atlanta Voice*, May 10, 2022, https://theatlantavoice.com/opinion-the-groundbreaking-and-complicated-life-of-mildred-fay-jefferson/.

[12]Nate Tinner-Williams, "Remembering Dolores B. Grier, Black Activist Against Abortion and Pioneering Diocesan Official," *Black Catholic Messenger*, February 16, 2023, www.blackcatholicmessenger.org/remembering-dolores-b-grier/.

[13]Franky V. Schaeffer, "Dr. Mildred Jefferson Speaking on a National Right to Life Committee video 1978," accessed December 29, 2024, https://radiancefoundation.org/trailblazer/.

[14]Tinner-Williams, "Remembering Dolores B. Grier."

[15]Dolores B. Grier, Pro-Life Women's News Conference, April 9, 1989, C-SPAN. www.c-span.org/program/news-conference/pro-life-women-news-conference/4345.

[16]William A. Jones, "How I Got Over," Episode Two: A Word in the Public Square, AND Campaign, February 8, 2024, video, 24:21, www.youtube.com/watch?v=ynEV_NveDwo&t=8s.

[17]Nannie H. Burroughs, *Nannie Helen Burroughs: A Documentary Portrait of an Early Civil Rights Pioneer 1900–1959*, ed. and annotated by Kelisha B. Graves (Notre Dame, IN: University of Notre Dame Press. 2019), 18.

[18]Kevin Allen, "Civil Right Pioneer Says Love Fueled the Movement," University of Notre Dame Law School, March 9, 2017, https://law.nd.edu/news-events/news/civil-rights-pioneer-says-love-fueled-the-movement/; "8 Greek Words for Love That Will Make Your Heart Soar," Dictionary.com, March 28, 2024, www.dictionary.com/e/greek-words-for-love/.

[19]Allen, "Civil Right Pioneer Says Love Fueled the Movement."

[20]Arthur E. Cundall and Leon Morris, *Judges and Ruth: An Introduction and Commentary*, vol. 7, *Tyndale Old Testament Commentaries* (Downers Grove, IL: InterVarsity Press, 1968), 106.

[21]Giuliana Grossi, "High Rates of Deaths of Despair Observed Among White Americans," *American Journal of Managed Care*, February 7, 2024, www.ajmc.com/view/high-rates-of-deaths-of-despair-observed-among-white-americans.

[22]Alden Whitman, "Mahalia Jackson, Gospel Singer, and a Civil Rights Symbol, Dies," *New York Times*, January 28, 1972, https://archive.nytimes.com/www.nytimes.com/learning/general/onthisday/bday/1026.html.

[23]Richard Rothstein, "The Soft Bigotry of High Expectation," Economic Policy Institute, January 30, 2024, www.epi.org/blog/the-soft-bigotry-of-high-expectations-to-combat-the-black-white-school-achievement-gap-remedy-persistent-segregation-dont-hope-for-miracle-teachers/.

[24]"A Wretch Like Me—The Story of John Newton (1725–1807)," Museum of the Bible, accessed December 18, 2024, www.museumofthebible.org/a-wretch-like-me.

[25]"A Wretch Like Me."

[26]Civilla D. Martin, "Why Should I Feel Discouraged, Why Should the Shadows Come," Hymnary.org, accessed Dec. 18, 2024, https://hymnary.org/text/why_should_i_feel_discouraged_why_should.

[27]Kastner Wilson, "On Partaking of the Divine Nature: Luther's Dependence on Augustine," *Andrews University Seminary Studies* 22, no. 1 (Spring 1984): 113–24, www.andrews.edu/library/car/cardigital/Periodicals/AUSS/1984-1/1984-1-12.pdf.